C000225594

9B

Dear John,
I send you this book published
by Laurence King on our office.
Hope you enjoy it.
With kind regards
OSCAR TORRESÓN

LVA
luis vidal + architects   www.luisvidal.com

Calle Velázquez 76   28001   Madrid   Spain
Calle de Los Navegantes   1912   Providencia   Santiago de

LUIS VIDAL + ARCHITECTS
FROM PROCESS TO RESULTS

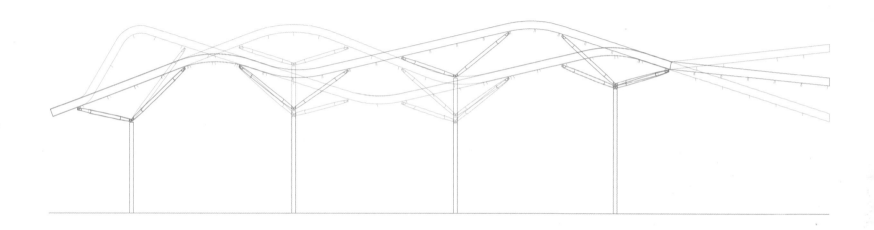

LUIS VIDAL + ARCHITECTS
FROM PROCESS TO RESULTS

CLARE MELHUISH
Creative Director Marta Cumellas

LAURENCE KING

Published in 2013
by Laurence King Publishing Ltd
361–373 City Road
London EC1V 1LR
United Kingdom
Tel: +44 20 7841 6900
Fax: +44 20 7841 6910
email: enquiries@laurenceking.com
www.laurenceking.com

Text © 2013 Clare Melhuish.

All rights reserved. No part of this publication may
be reproduced or transmitted in any form or by
any means, electronic or mechanical, including
photocopy, recording or any information storage and
retrieval system, without prior permission in writing
from the publisher.

A catalogue record for this book is available from
the British Library.

ISBN: 978-1-78067-290-8

Design: John Round Design
Printed in China

CONTENTS

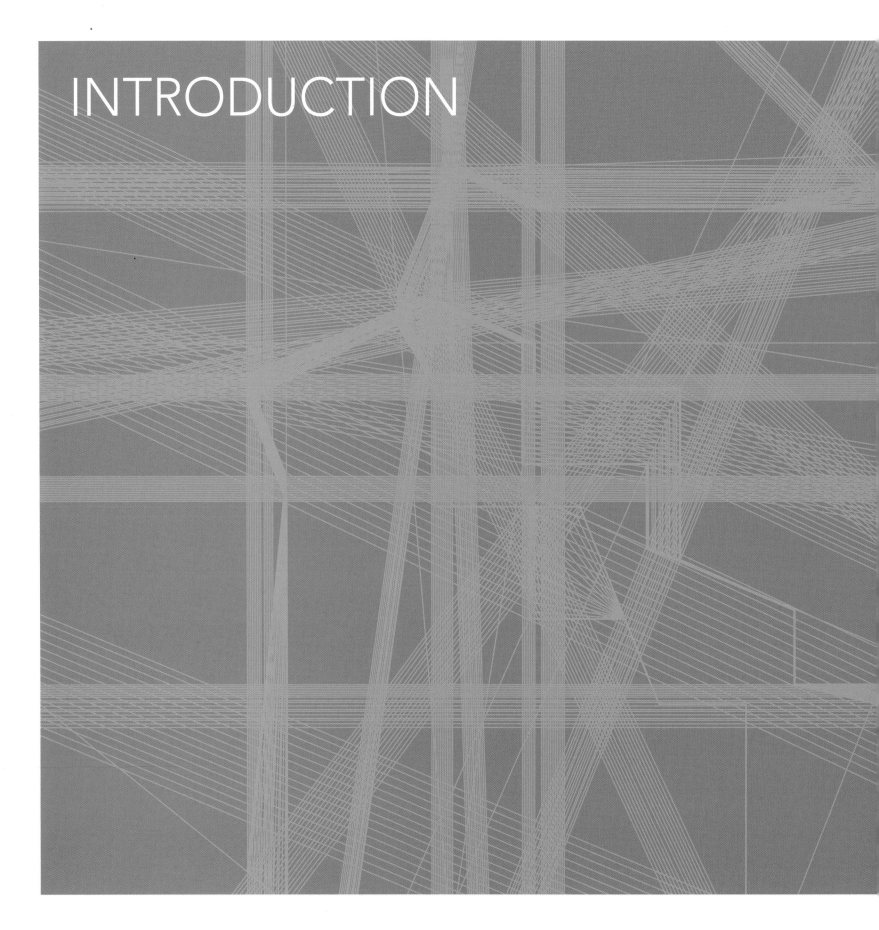

INTRODUCTION

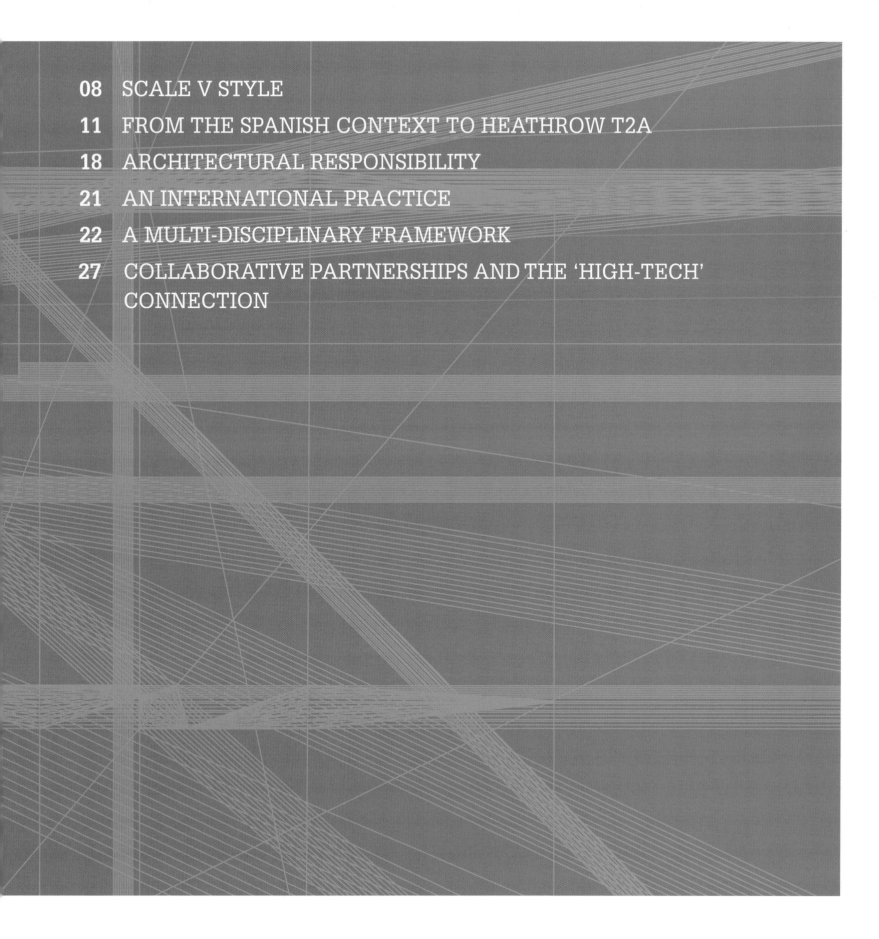

SCALE V STYLE

LVA is a practice which has established an architectural and professional identity on an international platform through its approach to scale and environmental responsibility as much as style. Founded in 2004 by Luis Vidal in Madrid, the core built and unbuilt projects during these eight years have been airports, masterplans and hospitals: the classic large-scale transport and healthcare hubs of the contemporary world, including the new Terminal 2A at London Heathrow. Yet while on the one hand these projects manifest that quality of sheer 'bigness', through a materialization of organizational process which may seem to transcend architectural style, LVA's work also extends to embrace the micro-scale and detail of everyday fittings and products such as chairs, doorhandles, taps and sanitaryware. Jumping from the very large to the very small scale, zooming in and out of perspective, it is an approach to design which is characterized, however, by a common insistence on the centrality of individual human experience in relation to everyday objects and spaces embedded in social processes. From the touch of smooth steel under the hand, to the view-in-motion through an international airport from check-in to security, or a hospital from reception to the ward or consultant's office, it is the personal perspective and emotional response invested in individual and relational identities which underpins the design imperative – even while working within the framework given by large organizations and multinational client bodies.

we give more for less LUIS VIDAL

Urbanism

Architecture

Design

jumping from the very large, to the very small scale, zooming in and out

⬆ embrace the micro-scale
LVA believe that whatever the size of the project, the design must be user-centred

➡ very large
The Valladolid masterplan is surgery to repair over 4km of city tissue
➡ see pages 148–151

⬆ individual human experience
This doorhandle can be held in two different ways. The prototype is covered in soft rubber

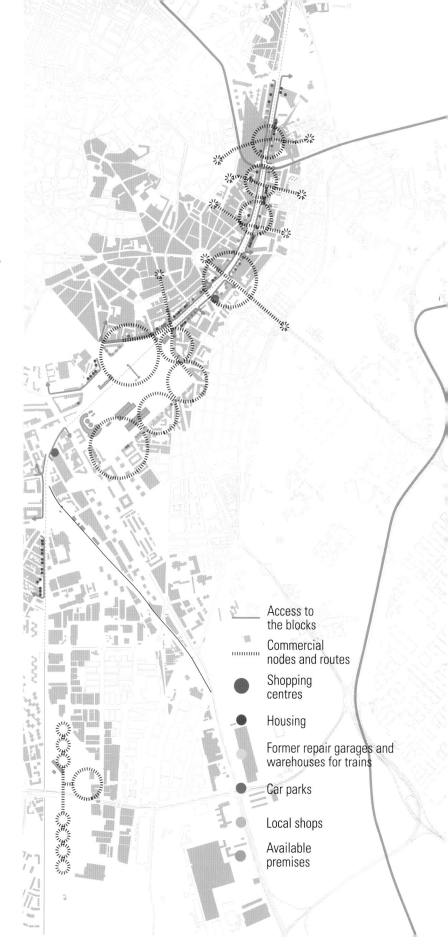

Access to the blocks

Commercial nodes and routes

Shopping centres

Housing

Former repair garages and warehouses for trains

Car parks

Local shops

Available premises

As a practice that has built its identity and workload in the first decade of the twenty-first century, LVA is one of a new generation of firms operating in a post-millennial architectural and social landscape. Preceded by a decade of millennium-inspired cultural monuments or 'grands projets', the new era, characterized by cumulative economic crisis, social fragmentation, and a climate of fear around national and personal security, has been witness to different types of initiative in architecture and construction. Patterns of mobility have intensified, as the need to connect and move around, both in virtual and real space, has been enforced by economic developments – as companies, people, chase after work and finance around the globe, from one place to the next. Transport infrastructure projects have moved high up the political agenda, providing the impetus for large-scale regeneration schemes, in which the significance of the building itself, as a formal, self-contained entity, has receded, and the network of transport nodes and hubs itself becomes

the generator of architectural ideas and form. Architects have been obliged to think and work on a larger (and smaller) scale, as one component of multi-faceted professional teams, within a collective framework of identity, answerable to multi-layered client bureaucracies. And opportunities in Europe have become circumscribed in the face of economic shrinkage, forcing architects more than ever before to think, connect and operate beyond the local, on a global stage, and within global networks of actors in the design and construction process.

⬆ practice
Project meeting at 9:19pm after a long day of work and before an even longer night

⬇ multi-faceted professional teams
Proposed methodology for the design of MOOD sanitaryware: LVA worked in close collaboration with Spanish client/ manufacturer NOKEN (Porcelanosa)
➔ see pages 208–209

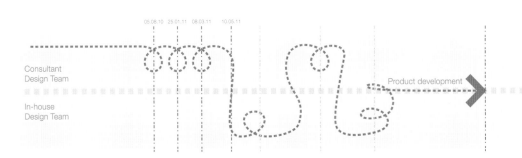

Consultant
Design Team

In-house
Design Team

Product development

05.08.10 25.01.11 08.03.11   10.05.11

FROM THE SPANISH CONTEXT TO HEATHROW T2A

The Spanish economy was booming from 1997, having pulled out of recession earlier in the decade, following the peak of the Barcelona Olympics and Seville Expo 1992 – both of which thrust contemporary Spanish architecture into the limelight on an international stage. An older generation of Spanish architects including Santiago Calatrava, Rafael Moneo, Ricardo Bofill and Enric Miralles, had established a strong and distinct aesthetic signature for Spanish architecture, through a range of high-profile projects – especially cultural and civic buildings, sports facilities and bridges, which captured the public imagination. In 2006, the Museum of Modern Art in New York staged a retrospective of contemporary Spanish architecture called 'On-Site'. Terence Riley, the Philip Johnson Chief Curator of Architecture and Design, wrote that

Spain was 'creating a mantle not of churches but of airports, museums, hospitals, libraries, train stations, stadiums and auditoriums'. He noted in the catalogue that 'Every region of the country boasts a wave of new works of architecture of the highest design ambition. Spain seems determined to correct the civil and cultural deficits that are a legacy not only of General Francisco Franco's military rule from 1939 to 1975 but also of the Counter-Reformation's mix of authoritarianism and religious orthodoxy.' He continued, 'Looking to recent history for clues to explain Spain's emergence as a laboratory for contemporary architecture, its hosting in 1992 of both the World's Fair in Seville and the 25th Olympiad in Barcelona was undoubtedly a catalyst. The previous year, the country had already taken a step toward the forefront of international architecture when the Basque government signed

→ train stations
A schematic design was needed for the Valladolid transportation hub in order to progress with the masterplanning

→ see pages 148–151

a leader has to have many virtues, and Luis has proved to have many of them: charisma, intelligence, persuasion, sensitivity and courage ARTURO BERNED

an agreement with the Solomon R. Guggenheim Museum in New York to finance and construct a museum in the aging industrial city of Bilbao. By the time of its completion six years later, to the acclaimed designs of Los Angeles architect Frank Gehry, Spain was also, like so many nations around the globe, self-consciously mapping its course for the next millennium through a number of ambitious architectural projects, such as the expansion and renovation of the venerable Museo del Prado by Rafael Moneo… and the vast City of Arts and Sciences in Valencia by locally born Santiago Calatrava.' (Riley 2006)

In fact, 'On-Site' included two buildings designed by Vidal – the MNCARS Restaurant interior, and Terminal 4 at Madrid's Barajas Airport, a collaboration with the Richard Rogers Partnership (renamed Rogers Stirk Harbour + Partners in 2007, referred to hereon as RSHP) implemented by Vidal while at Estudio Lamela Arquitectos (ELA), and awarded the RIBA Stirling Prize in 2006. But in March 2004, eight days before LVA set up in business, the terrorist bomb attack on Atocha railway station in Madrid threw the country into a state of shock. Three days after the atrocity, a general election resulted in the formation of a socialist minority government. For a year the country existed in a state of paralysis, and architectural work dried up. Then, LVA won four major competitions in a row, including Zaragoza Airport, commissioned for the Zaragoza Expo, and Infanta Leonor Hospital in the Vallecas district of the capital, part of an ambitious political project to build seven new hospitals in the city at

← MNCARS Restaurant
The existing space by Jean Nouvel was very imposing and LVA established a dialogue by using straight lines and white structures that appear to be floating
→ see pages 198–199

↑ Zaragoza Airport

3D render of the competition-winning entry

← Mock-up of a module from the soffit of the new London Heathrow Terminal 2A

once. The practice took off; its growth from that point occurred during the same period that Spanish companies such as the bank Santander and the building contractor Ferrovial established themselves as global brands through notable overseas acquisitions, while establishing the Spanish brand itself as quintessentially European, youthful and dynamic. Those qualities are reflected in the growth of LVA as a young, very professional, European architectural firm with an international outlook; and one which promises high-quality, functional, but non-rhetorical architecture as a framework for the enjoyment of everyday life, and the enhancement of individual well-being within the complex processes of contemporary society.

In 2014, LVA will see its Terminal 2A at Heathrow open to the public after years of hard work, during which the office has been split between two sites in Madrid and London. Following on from the successful collaboration on the competition-winning scheme (1997: RRP/ELA) for Madrid Airport's dramatic Terminal 4 building, with its striking processions of rainbow-coloured, tree-shaped columns and calm, spacious atmosphere, LVA won and completed

⊙ Terminal 2A at Heathrow
Structural work on T2A began summer 2010. Image taken winter 2010

#BARAJAS we needed a functional airport, not a beautiful building; combining both aspects was the key to success JOSÉ MANUEL HESSE

◐ ⬆ airport terminal at Zaragoza
The original brief asked for the extension of the existing building, which can just be seen at the left of the new terminal. LVA challenged the brief and won the competition
→ see pages 168–171

⬆ size
The LVA / RSHP team in Madrid in 2008, in a photograph taken from the building opposite the office

⬇ approaching the Richard Rogers Partnership
Vidal has written Richard Rogers' biography for Spanish magazine *ARTE*

work in 2008 on a 'little brother' for Barajas T4, a new airport terminal at Zaragoza, which was a finalist for the Mies van der Rohe Prize 2009. Heathrow Terminal 2A, for client Ferrovial, will be a fitting successor, then, to these first two projects, and provide a symbol for LVA's association with London and its unique position at the intersection of Spanish and Anglo-Saxon traditions and practices of architecture and urban design.

It is this position and outlook – along with its size – which distinguishes the practice from others in Spain, where the small-scale, studio-based model continues to be dominant. Vidal's own architectural education and training took place in London, where at 25 he became the youngest overseas

architect ever to be invited to join the Royal Institute of British Architects. His years at Thames Polytechnic (now Greenwich University), which he chose for its balanced approach to the technical, humanistic and artistic dimensions of architecture, provided the foundations of an understanding of British architectural culture, technique and professional practice. Returning to Spain to work in practice during the 1990s felt, he has said, like 'turning the clock back 20 years', and he set himself to revolutionizing the working practices he encountered, in the light of an international outlook, which included approaching the Richard Rogers Partnership in 1997 to work on the high-profile Barajas project competition.

ARCHITECTURAL RESPONSIBILITY

A decade later, LVA itself has established an international identity, through a portfolio characterized less by flashy landmark architecture than big, extendable buildings – notably airports and hospitals – which organize complex processes of human mobility, circulation and interaction into coherent, negotiable built landscapes of social practice.

In 2011, the practice was invited to exhibit its work at the European Parliament building in Brussels, and issued a public statement regarding the ambitions for this work, titled 'Collective Responsibility in Europe':

'Artists create and transmit emotions through sculptures and paintings of unpredictable result. Engineers resolve technology within known parameters and tools, a predictable result. Architects must master both professions in order to deliver useful environments to society, whether it be a city, building or chair.

- Architects have to apply a correct balance between tradition and modernity, as they respond to a society but play a role in its progress, contributing to welfare.
- Architects are adventurers, as design is one of the greatest adventures of life. You simply set out without knowing where your journey will take you to.

exhibit
A significant group of LVA's architects and working partners went to Brussels for the official opening

European Parliament HQ
The exhibition was based on video projections and models

This is the process, as important and intensive as the end result.

- Architects have to exercise between innovation and technique, as innovation is in the terrain of the unknown and technique is in the terrain of the known.
- Architects must practise with precision, as they have to please society, clients and users. They have to manage expectations, both functional and aesthetic. They have to deliver quality, both artistic and technical.
- Architects have a great responsibility, as the shape of cities, buildings and design have an influence on the way society performs, behaves and acts.
- Architects have a demanding profession; they walk on a knife's edge, as they cannot fail in their design; otherwise all society will have to "live with it" viewing "that big mistake" for years.
- Architects are a strange breed; they are both unpredictable and predictable. They stand and fight for their ideals.'

(Luis Vidal, European Parliament HQ, 3rd May 2011)

twenty-five years a colleague. Intellect, output, integrity. Able to direct diverse personalities and skills to deliver unique solutions RAY HOLE

AN INTERNATIONAL PRACTICE

Luis Vidal's final-year project as an architecture student in London (1994) was a scheme for City Airport in Docklands, following work on a masterplan for the headquarters of GATT (now the World Trade Organization) by the Thames Barrier, with his friend and fellow student Ray Hole. The project included a high-speed rail station at Charlton (1993), inspired by the new high-speed rail station built for the Seville Expo in Spain (1992), and a port at the Thames Barrier. It was the culmination of a period of training during which he was drawn to focus on airports and transportation schemes, a field which he understood would be one of significant growth in the future, and that he believed could be infused with an experience of greater enjoyment on the part of the travelling public. At the same time he came into contact with a number of British architects and engineers who helped to form his particular outlook on architectural practice – among them John Winter, Tony Hunt and Neil Spiller. His tutor, John Lyall (of John Lyall Architects; formerly co-founder of Alsop and Lyall with Will Alsop), whom Vidal contemplated joining in practice after qualifying, recalls the innovation and ambition which distinguished his work, and underpins LVA's commitment to an international platform of practice, characterized by projects that assemble transnational trajectories of movement and mobility, by sea, air and rail. Strategies for dealing with transport infrastructure, circulation patterns, connections and extensions programme the work and set it apart from a static, self-contained architecture of monumentality and symbolic representation.

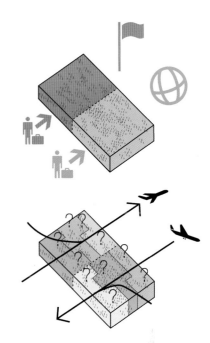

⬆ transportation schemes
Two kinds of segregation occur in secured transportation nodes: between domestic and international travellers and between departures and arrivals

⬅ focus on airports
In a building the size of T2A, different construction teams work in different parts of the building simultaneously

➡ circulation patterns
The study of the transportation links to Campus Palmas Altas (CPA) in Seville showed the need for a pedestrian and bike connection to the city centre

➔ see pages 172–177

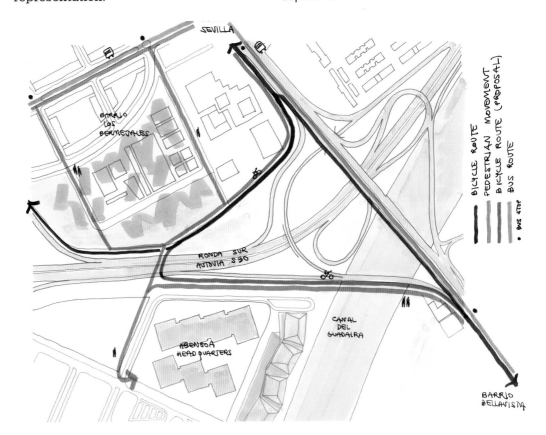

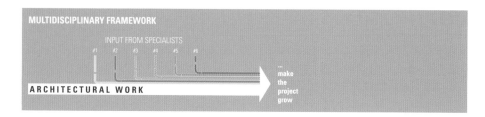

MULTIDISCIPLINARY FRAMEWORK

INPUT FROM SPECIALISTS

#1 #2 #3 #4 #5 #6

ARCHITECTURAL WORK

... make the project grow

⬆ multi-disciplinary framework
Incorporating technical issues into the
design is seen as value-adding and an
enriching process

⬇ multi-disciplinary framework
In LVA, the specialists' work informs the
architectural project in the same way
that the architects' work informs the
specialists' project

MULTIDISCIPLINARY MANAGEMENT

Standard Practice:
"Architects **decide**, Specialists **follow**"

Architectural Project

Specialists

LVA's Formula.
"Project **grows** with the specialists' feedback"

Architectural Project

Project coordination
and feedback

Specialists

⬇ In LVA / RSHP Madrid, working space runs
through two century-old residential buildings
in the Salamanca neighbourhood. The original
structure of the space can still be read

A MULTI-DISCIPLINARY FRAMEWORK

The need to balance the art of architecture with technical values, expertise and efficiency, within a multi-disciplinary framework of practice, drives the work of LVA, and sets it outside the so-called 'starchitect' system in which single-name practices produce landmark buildings as authored, aesthetized statements within urban landscapes and regeneration programmes driven by a culture of branding and the concept of the 'experience economy' (Lonsway 2009). 'Starchitects' are perceived to provide added value to regeneration schemes, by creating stylistically recognizable architectural forms within a global hierarchy of urban skylines, and as a backdrop to international events, which also contribute to the location of cities on a global investment map. But, as the anthropologist Judith Okely has noted, 'brand-named architects' often work in a comparable manner to 'some celebrity millionaires and conceptual artists [who] dream up and patent an idea then employ craft workers or mere labourers to realize it as object' (Marcus and Okely 2007: 359). The concept of the international practice,

balance in architecture is achieved when the team is able to read the signs that will make the project unique

JUAN ANTONIO CANTALAPIEDRA

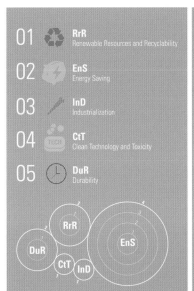

01	♻	**RrR** Renewable Resources and Recyclability
02	⚡	**EnS** Energy Saving
03	💉	**InD** Industrialization
04	TECH	**CtT** Clean Technology and Toxicity
05	🕐	**DuR** Durability

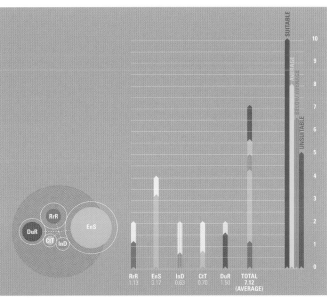

| | RrR 1.13 | EnS 3.17 | InD 0.63 | CtT 0.70 | DuR 1.50 | TOTAL 7.12 (AVERAGE) |

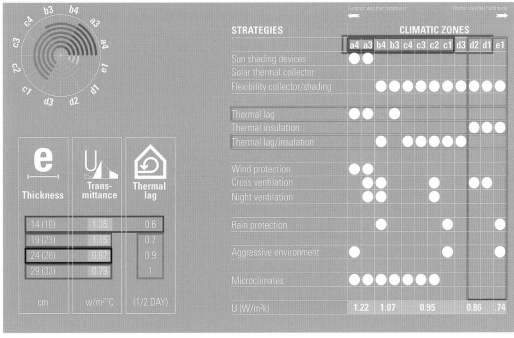

	e Thickness	**U** Trans-mittance	**🏠** Thermal lag
	14 (18)	1.35	0.6
	19 (23)	1.15	0.7
	24 (28)	0.87	0.9
	29 (33)	0.79	1
	cm	w/m²°C	(1/2 DAY)

STRATEGIES	CLIMATIC ZONES											
	a4	a3	b4	b3	c4	c3	c2	c1	d3	d2	d1	e1
Sun shading devices	●	●										
Solar thermal collector												
Flexibility collector/shading			●	●	●	●	●	●	●	●	●	●
Thermal lag	●	●		●								
Thermal insulation										●	●	●
Thermal lag/insulation				●	●	●	●	●	●			
Wind protection	●	●										
Cross ventilation		●	●				●			●	●	
Night ventilation		●	●				●					
Rain protection				●				●			●	
Aggressive environment	●						●				●	
Microclimates	●	●	●	●	●	●	●					
U (W/m²k)	1.22		1.07		0.95				0.86		.74	

Summer weather harshness — *Winter weather harshness*

by contrast, evokes the large multi-disciplinary firms that grew during the 1960s and 1970s to tackle the continuing postwar challenges of reconstruction, infrastructure planning, and large-scale urban extension and reconfiguration around the world. British practices in particular, such as Arup, Llewelyn-Davies, RMJM, YRM and BDP – known by acronyms rather than the individual names of founding partners – assembled professional expertise and experience under one umbrella, and established a benchmark for international consultancy and practice management embodied in major functional masterplanning projects and complex buildings such as hospitals, universities and airports, in the various locations around the world to which they exported their technical and design services. As the economic and political landscape changed, the same firms began to transfer their expertise into the corporate and commercial sector, where they began to compete alongside the large-scale American practices such as SOM, HOK, KPF and Gensler for international projects.

LVA is [one of] the largest of five comparable practices on the

⬅ assembled professional expertise
Arup's Madrid office façade department has been working closely with LVA in their façade research and development project

➡ see pages 156–157

one day the client sees
the finished building and
says to the architect: now
I understand what you
were saying. It is difficult
to explain space with
drawings and words!

MARCOS VELASCO

Pedestrian access to the CPA office complex in Seville

↑ warm and personal
Working environment in the shared offices of
LVA / RSHP on Calle Velázquez, Madrid

↑ Spanish flavour
Vidal on an office trip to Valladolid, in the
heart of the Ribera del Duero wine area

Spanish architectural landscape,
at around 80 staff at the time of
writing. Half its work is undertaken
for construction companies, and
it regularly works in joint-venture
partnerships. The perception of its
standing as an international practice,
with a professional, pragmatic, multi-
disciplinary outlook in this tradition,
and a hybrid Iberian and Anglo-Saxon
profile, has attracted a multinational
community of architects to work in its
Madrid and London offices alongside
the core Spanish contingent. German,
Italian, Portuguese, American, Japanese
and English staff make up the numbers
on close-knit project teams led and
co-ordinated by project directors, and
broaden the scope of reference beyond
the immediate Spanish context, building
the practice's trajectory across an
international stage, and particularly

towards the emerging markets for
architectural services in areas such
as South America. Yet at the same
time it has succeeded in retaining the
atmosphere of a large 'family' – a term
used repeatedly by different members
of the office to describe its ambience. It
offers staff flexibility in moving from one
project to another, and opportunities for
personal and professional development
that are not necessarily available in
other practices, many of which have
more rigid approaches to structural
organization. The atmosphere in
the office is described as warm and
personal, with a close relationship
between Vidal himself, the directors
and staff, which maintains 'the Spanish
flavour of doing things', and contrasts
with the anonymity and standardization
of working processes common to large
international practices.

COLLABORATIVE PARTNERSHIPS AND THE 'HIGH-TECH' CONNECTION

Part of the reason for LVA's success in establishing an international platform for its work is the fact that it has been willing to engage in active collaborations, not only with construction companies and other consultants, but also with other internationally established architectural practices such as Rogers Stirk Harbour + Partners in London (on projects such as the Valladolid masterplan and the offices for Abengoa in Seville, which won a RIBA Award and is also the first LEED Platinum building in Europe) and Renzo Piano in Genoa (on the Botín Centre in Santander). One of the intermediate design phases of Heathrow Terminal 2A was another collaboration with a high-profile practice, Foster + Partners, first in Madrid and then in London.

Vidal has always been interested in the idea of the group or team in architectural history, as a platform for exchanging ideas – for example, the Bauhaus, or Team X. As he says, 'one plus one can add up to more than two.' But these particular linkages point to an attraction to the British 'High-Tech' tradition, which reflects Vidal's own interest in technology and engineering. Growing out of a history of native engineering expertise exemplified in the work of Isambard Kingdom Brunel and powered by early industrial development, High-Tech emerged in the 1960s and 1970s through the transforming influence of Buckminster

T4 + Chicago + London = challenges = discussions + questions + ideas + solutions. In time = creation + vision + innovation + experience = LVA FERNANDO CALLEJÓN

↑ Rogers Stirk Harbour + Partners
Luis Vidal and Simon Smithson – RSHP's director in Spain – together at the office

↑ Renzo Piano
Design review meeting at the Renzo Piano Building Workshop in Genoa, Italy

⬅ bridges
Corten and stainless steel combined in this
pedestrian bridge at the CPA, Seville
➡ see pages 204–205

Fuller, Cedric Price and Archigram, as
a technologically driven architecture
characterized by indeterminacy,
flexibility and social idealism. Piano
and Rogers' Pompidou Centre in Paris
(1972–77) is described by Kenneth
Frampton as 'the paradigm of this
movement… an outstanding popular
success… [and] a brilliant tour de force
in advanced technique… with minimum
regard for the specificity of its brief'
(Frampton 1980: 285). The translation
of an original industrial, structural and
functional vocabulary dedicated to the
design of bridges and other elements of
infrastructure to the design of forward-
looking manufacturing, cultural and
office buildings in the post-industrial
era generated its own architectural
aesthetic. It celebrated the technical
and functional bases of architecture
in a manner at once playful, romantic
and serious about the need to develop
an energy-efficient, environmentally
sustainable architecture for future

generations. At the same time, such buildings offered a new language for architectural projects which transcended narrowly defined national and cultural identities and took up a position on a transnational stage – whether in the form of arts centres or airports.

Prior to setting up his own practice, Vidal was headhunted and offered, among other jobs, the chance to establish an architectural department in the Spanish engineering firm Sener, which specializes in naval and aeronautical design and subsequently partnered LVA on the Zaragoza Airport project.

LVA's work demonstrates the inspiration of British engineers such as Tony Hunt; but it may also be viewed in relation to the British High-Tech tradition, in the sense that it marshals an array of expertise to produce technologically driven projects which also set out to introduce a dimension of playfulness, enjoyment and well-being to the experience of those who will occupy the spaces. Fundamental to that, it also displays a level of environmental responsibility and performance that sets a new standard in Spanish architecture, and a commitment to exploring a brief

⬆ Zaragoza Airport
The supporting structure of the roof is centred on the modules. This allows for a better reading of the space's geometry

Luis understands the world as one unified system; with each project he feels a responsibility to keep the planet in mind JANET KAFKA

in close collaboration with client and building managers. On completing his architectural training in Greenwich, Vidal had considered joining John Lyall's new practice, attracted by the use of technology that characterized Lyall's previous work with Will Alsop – although Vidal was less at ease with the more extravagant aspects of their formal approach. As it was, he returned to Spain to take up a position with Estudio Lamela Arquitectos, with whom he had worked during his post-Part 1 year out (1991), and who had approached him during his Diploma year to work on a competition for a new headquarters building for AENA, the Spanish airport authority, which they won. Vidal subsequently oversaw the expansion of the practice to 150 staff, developing a range of international work in airport design; this provided the opportunity to approach the Richard Rogers Partnership to collaborate on the competition for Madrid Terminal 4, marking the beginning of a long-standing collaborative relationship between the Rogers office and his own, which is represented by their shared office space in the Salamanca neighbourhood of Madrid.

As Vidal says, there is always creative 'ego' at stake in any creative partnership, but he does not believe it has to present an obstruction to successful collaborative working arrangements with other architects who have established a profile over long careers spanning many decades, and share a certain outlook in terms of the importance of functionality, sustainability and enjoyment as the foundation of architectural expression. In particular, his prior understanding of the British approach to architectural culture and practice rendered the new practice open and responsive to other, complementary ways of working. Simon Smithson, director of RSHP's Madrid office, has defined it as 'a special skill of being able to work with us, understand what we wanted and translate that into, be a bridge to, the Spanish way of working which is different... very different as a culture... It's based on personal contacts, good people skills, and being insistent and finding a way to talk to the right person... Relationships

🔽 work with us
Vidal, Rogers and their Madrid office's teams in 2006

🔼 long-standing collaborative relationship
A working model of the Valladolid masterplan measuring 3m by 1m, and made at LVA / RSHP's office out of foamboard, balsa wood and an aerial photograph. Simple yet very effective

🔙 long-standing collaborative relationship
The Campus Palmas Altas (CPA) project was won by LVA / RSHP in an open international competition
➡ see pages 172–177

are very one-to-one… But Luis understood both [ways of working], the strengths and weaknesses of both… he was able to mediate, and realize when one side had a point which was valid and needed translating to the other side' (SS, in conversation, 29.03.12).

As Smithson points out, 'you're not educated in school to think about collaborations… But now there are so many things changing… Technology changes every five years and, in the context in which we all have to operate… collaborations are more and more important.' At the time that Vidal brokered the relationship between RRP and ELA, this type of collaborative partnership was a relatively new phenomenon for RRP but Smithson says 'it gave us courage to go and pursue collaborations in other parts of the world.' A large part of the reason

for its success was that 'there was a willingness to collaborate on a project rather than a design… everyone wanted to do the best possible airport they could, that was the object' (SS); the people on the team had to 'feel part of the project rather than one or other of the offices'. Vidal himself played a central role in that process, with what Richard Rogers has described as 'a unique ability to mix and exchange ideas… He enables things, he is a catalyst.' That role 'becomes very important – enabling the rest of the team to function' (SS).

Following 15 years of working together, there is what Smithson describes as 'a lot of common ground' between the two offices, and 'without a common ground there's no exchange of ideas.' But it also depends on an investment of time and effort in

making the relationship last, and an understanding, as Rogers stresses, that 'teamwork is crucial in architecture'. It is that, rather than the pursuit of individual design identity, which has allowed LVA to develop and grow as 'a remarkably collaborative office' (SS), and expand its perspective beyond the immediate Spanish context in which it is embedded.

One of the benefits of this style of working is the access it generates to international networks of clients, contractors and consultants, nurtured by the practice's communications department, through the medium of the office's particular expertise in the areas of hospitals, airports and masterplanning, and its emphasis on the principle of environmental responsibility. Óscar Torrejón, Partner, believes that LVA is well positioned to 'offer big architecture with a friendly

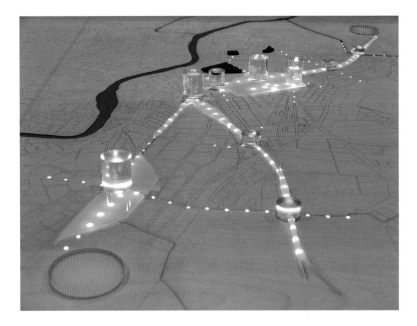

⬆ willingness to collaborate on a project
The Valladolid project was on public display for a month. This model shows the new proposed nodes of activity for the city, which complement the existing ones
➔ see pages 148–151

⬆ ability to mix and exchange ideas
Smithson, Vidal and Rogers in a design meeting at the Valladolid office, in 2006

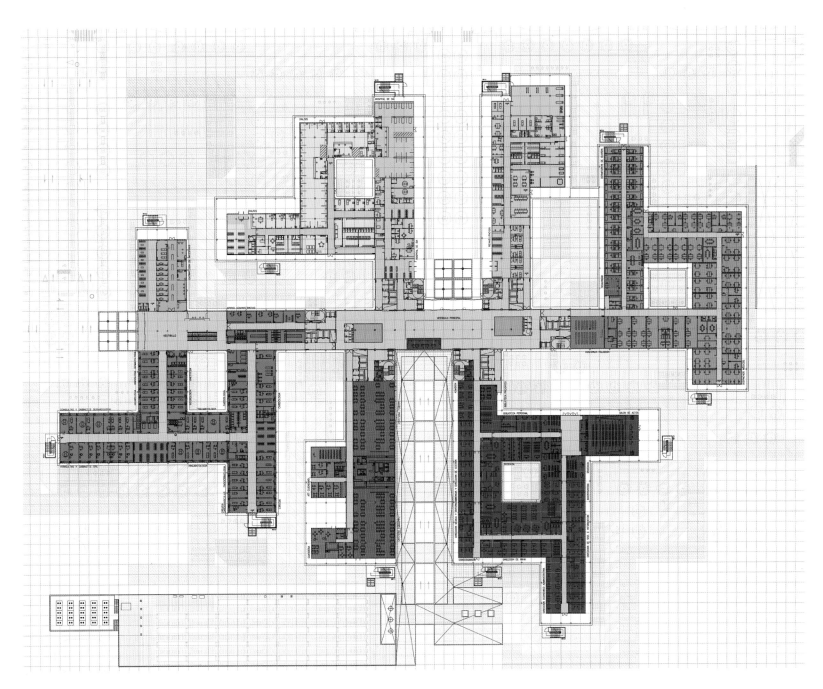

feeling', without transforming itself into a very large, more impersonal business, through its ability to 'balance different aspects of what we do'. In addition, the basis of the practice's work in buildings driven by very precise and specialized functional programmes means that it is compelled to work with other consultants, to be open to the knowledge that other parties bring to the design process, and through that dissemination of expertise engage in a process of continuous learning which ultimately strengthens the aesthetic argument on any project, but also supports the client's priority for a successful, workable architectural solution to a particular set of problems and relationships.

⬆ specialized functional programmes
Designed from scratch, Infanta Leonor Hospital's shape responds to the needs of a twenty-first-century hospital

→ see pages 178–181

#CAN MISSES HOSPITAL the skin is inspired by Ibiza's vernacular architecture. The challenge: to create a building from the place for the place, but with twenty-first-century resources DAVID ÁVILA

Notwithstanding the link with RSHP, and through that, perhaps, the High-Tech aesthetic, there are no presumptions about style as such in the office – nor about structures or techniques: 'we are very open-minded,' says Vidal, commenting on the fact that clients can be surprised when told the architects on a project don't know in advance what a façade is going to be made of, or how it is going to look. There is an active concern with the definition and evolution of a proper 'Mediterranean' architecture, based on appropriate environmental and aesthetic principles designed to meet those particular climatic conditions, seen particularly in LVA's work on projects such as the Can Misses Hospital in Ibiza. And there is always a commitment to innovation, in the vanguard of technique, in order to produce 'added value' on any project. But although the office is interested in the latest construction technologies and the principles of modular architecture, the application

⬆ Can Misses Hospital
Can Misses Hospital is very close to the historic city of Ibiza

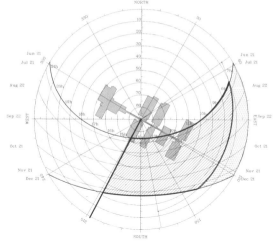

⬆ particular climatic conditions
Study of the path of the sun over Can Misses Hospital

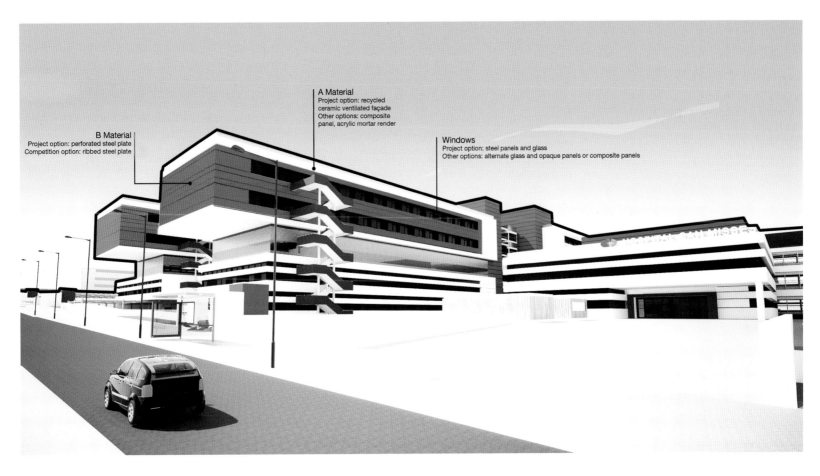

B Material
Project option: perforated steel plate
Competition option: ribbed steel plate

A Material
Project option: recycled ceramic ventilated façade
Other options: composite panel, acrylic mortar render

Windows
Project option: steel panels and glass
Other options: alternate glass and opaque panels or composite panels

⬆ Can Misses Hospital
The façade is designed to minimize overheating from direct sunlight

⬇ no presumptions about style
Night view of the short façades of Can Misses Hospital's satellites. LVA's competition-winning internal design is by María Astiaso

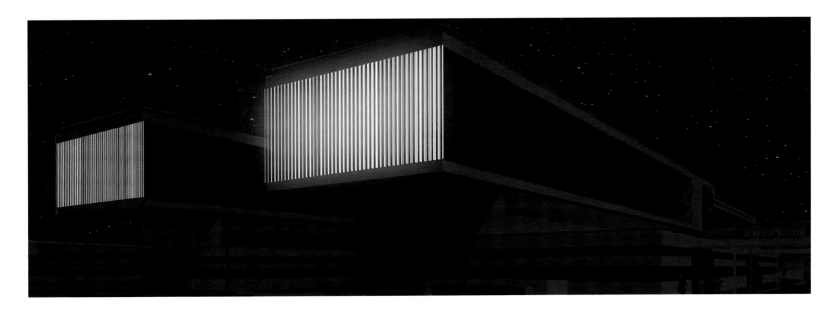

of industrialized architectural systems
and solutions to projects in Spain
is not always possible, because the
resources to achieve a sophisticated
technological approach are not always
available – and sometimes the most
efficient solution to an architectural brief
in Spain is not the most industrialized
one. In short, the office has no set of
standard approaches or approved design
methods to be applied to each project as
it comes in. Similarly, there is no ready
set of architectural references to be
drawn on by the office as a consistent
framework for spatial and formal
development. Rather, an open-minded
approach to design, based on principles
of orientation, flexibility, texture and
colour – and reflected in the diversity
of graphic expression through which
architectural intent is investigated and
communicated – remains the norm, and
allows individual members of the office
to make their own contribution to its
identity in different ways that reflect their
various backgrounds and routes to LVA.

⬇ industrialized architectural systems
For the Vigo Hospital project, LVA had
to convince the client that dry façade
construction was the best option

➔ see pages 188–193

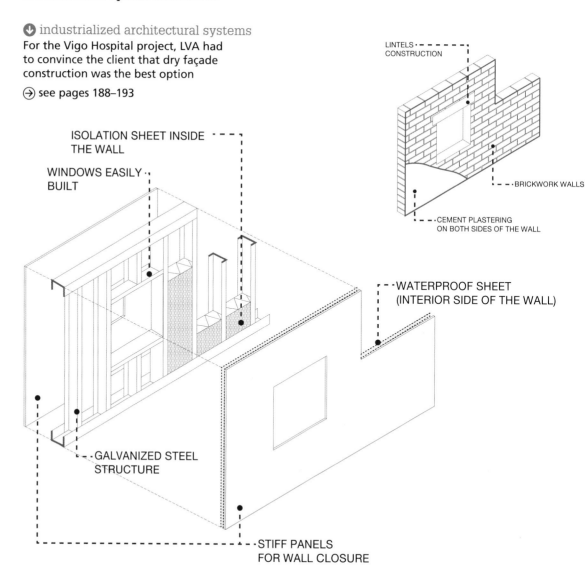

LINTELS
CONSTRUCTION

BRICKWORK WALLS

CEMENT PLASTERING
ON BOTH SIDES OF THE WALL

ISOLATION SHEET INSIDE
THE WALL

WINDOWS EASILY
BUILT

WATERPROOF SHEET
(INTERIOR SIDE OF THE WALL)

GALVANIZED STEEL
STRUCTURE

STIFF PANELS
FOR WALL CLOSURE

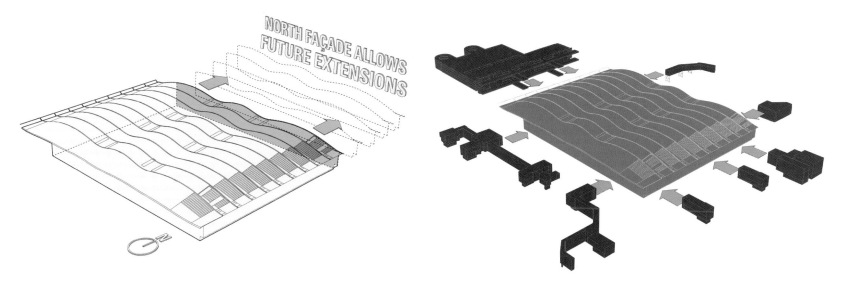

↑ open-minded approach to design
Concept for future expansion of T2A at Heathrow

↓ open-minded approach to design
One of the starting points for the roof concept of T2A was the wing structure of the first successful powered aircraft, the Wright Flyer

↑ open-minded approach to design
Formal concept for T2A, with secondary uses treated as independent shapes plugged onto the main volume

DESIGN AS AN OPEN-ENDED PROCESS

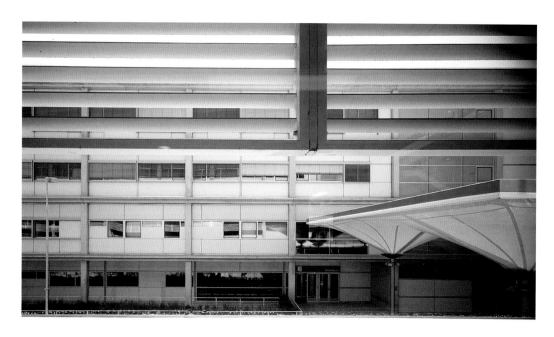

Infanta Leonor Hospital
Entrances to Infanta Leonor Hospital lead straight to the distribution spine for ease of orientation

Views across the ward blocks in Infanta Leonor Hospital

see pages 178–181

A HYBRID TYPOLOGY: ARCHITECTURE AS SERVICE TO THE PUBLIC

When LVA won the competition for Infanta Leonor Hospital in Madrid, it seemed to be a sector that could easily be improved – one where some extra value could readily be offered to lift the standard of an uninspiring building typology. As a green-coded architect (see page 115) from the office comments, most hospitals at the time seemed like 'hostile environments' for patients and staff alike. And it was airport design that provided the key to an approach that LVA believed could work – an approach based on a creative handling of issues around circulation, mobility and careful segregation of functions and user groups designed to generate a 'healing architecture' to enhance well-being in the hospital environment. Rather than treating these large, complex, technical buildings simply as 'working machines', as perceived by many big clients and contractors, the office applied knowledge derived from dialogue with hospital managers, doctors, airport directors and staff to refine the development of the design within the framework of the client's specifications for areas, layouts and cost. It was thus that the office's theory of 'airport-hospitals' was born, challenging a typology-led approach to architectural design by blurring the

healing architecture
Concepts behind LVA's hospital design

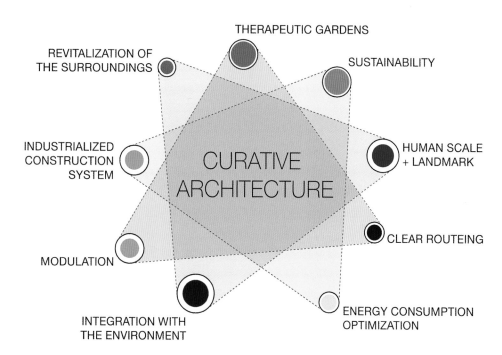

REVITALIZATION OF THE SURROUNDINGS

THERAPEUTIC GARDENS

SUSTAINABILITY

INDUSTRIALIZED CONSTRUCTION SYSTEM

CURATIVE ARCHITECTURE

HUMAN SCALE + LANDMARK

MODULATION

CLEAR ROUTEING

INTEGRATION WITH THE ENVIRONMENT

ENERGY CONSUMPTION OPTIMIZATION

boundaries both of a well-established architectural classification system and, if you like, a typology of users.

Airport users and hospital users tend to be conceived of in very different ways – the former as fit, active, busy holidaymakers or business travellers; the latter as sick, vulnerable and anxious patients. But from LVA's perspective, both groups are framed as vulnerable to stress, anxiety and exposure in the process of negotiating a complicated sequential transit from arrival to departure, involving multiple layers of third-party intervention and personal examination. The physical framework for this process has much in common in both cases, characterized by very large-scale construction, elaborate subdivision of space, a reliance on strategic signage and instruction to guide people smoothly through the process from start to finish in an uninterrupted flow, and a strict organizational segregation of vetted and non-vetted (or 'clean' and 'dirty',

in airport-design jargon) staff and public, which is reflected in the spatial management of the building and closely monitored points of contact. In addition, there is often a requirement for built-in flexibility and growth, allowing for future alteration and expansion as user numbers increase over time. But above all, both typologies of building/event/user are understood as embodying complex, stratified social worlds of heterogeneous publics brought together in one place for a variably specified period of time – and all those individuals are regarded by LVA as potential beneficiaries of a better quality of physical and psychological experience for the duration of their visit.

Vidal has always approached architecture as 'a public service or a service to the public', as he puts it. The world requires 'more ordered structures', he suggests, to cope with increasing social and economic pressures, and the demand for minimization of risk

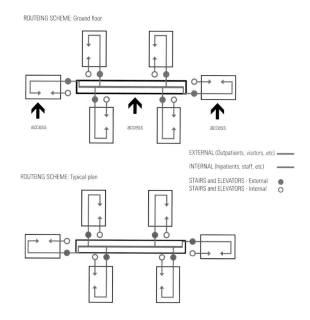

ROUTEING SCHEME: Ground floor

ROUTEING SCHEME: Typical plan

EXTERNAL (Outpatients, visitors, etc) ——
INTERNAL (Inpatients, staff, etc) ——
STAIRS and ELEVATORS - External ●
STAIRS and ELEVATORS - Internal ○

⬆ strict organizational segregation
In hospitals, staff and inpatients use different circulation routes from visitors and outpatients

⬇ 'clean' and 'dirty'
At airports, the 'clean' area is on 'airside', which is accessible only to passengers and staff who have passed through security controls

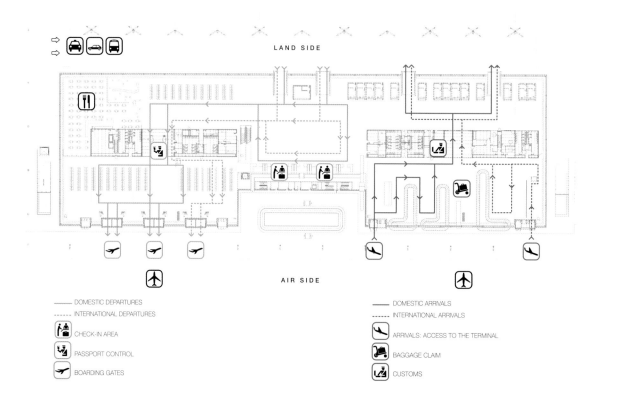

LAND SIDE

AIR SIDE

—— DOMESTIC DEPARTURES
----- INTERNATIONAL DEPARTURES
CHECK-IN AREA
PASSPORT CONTROL
BOARDING GATES

—— DOMESTIC ARRIVALS
----- INTERNATIONAL ARRIVALS
ARRIVALS: ACCESS TO THE TERMINAL
BAGGAGE CLAIM
CUSTOMS

TERMINAL ROOF EMBRACES THREE DAY-LIT PROCESSING SPACES AND CONNECTIVITY

CHECK-IN   SECURITY   GATES

DEPARTURES
ARRIVALS

◄ maximization of security
T2A needs to be able to be adapted very quickly to changes in security policies

▼ enhancing the public's experience
Ways in which an LVA-designed hospital improves user experience

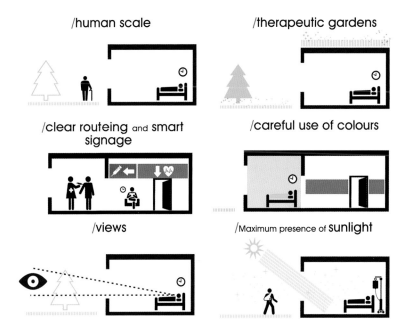

/human scale

/therapeutic gardens

/clear routeing and smart signage

/careful use of colours

/views

/Maximum presence of sunlight

and maximization of security, while enhancing the public's experience of well-being in ever more complex social processes. In design terms, he argues, these factors demand a responsive rather than prescriptive approach, and architects should present themselves as 'allies who add value' rather than combatants in a war over aesthetics and architectural ideology. The architect then needs to engage with client and public, adopting an open outlook, as an enabler for the best possible project that can be achieved within the framework proposed, subject to its re-evaluation through the design process and to any expertise that the architect can offer. Staff members working on Heathrow Terminal 2A define it as a 'logical approach', rather than the pursuit of a particular architectural brand or look,

free of predetermined parameters as to how a design might develop. It embodies a lack of fear with regard to engaging with the nuts and bolts of a building, and a reluctance to hide or aestheticize the technical specification, which manifests a relish for solving particular problems through well-engineered solutions. The field of airport and hospital design represents, then, a rich opportunity for implementing technological expertise as a service to the public, which may not guarantee iconic buildings (though some are), or architectural stardom, but opens challenging possibilities of providing 'more for less' – citing Vidal's variation on Mies van der Rohe's celebrated aphorism, 'less is more' – to a mass audience.

A PRAGMATIC APPROACH

As various critics from within the social sciences have observed, the professional mythology of the architect as inspired artist and creative genius (such as Mies van der Rohe himself), and conceiver of iconic structures, is one that needs to be balanced by an understanding of the reality of architectural practice and construction, especially in its modern and contemporary forms, as a collective effort involving a wide range of different parties to the design process, a vast number of different interactions in different contexts and geographical locations, and many different tools and technologies, which also have an impact on the outcome. Not only that, but buildings have lives beyond the point where the keys are handed over to the occupant, and may evolve in unexpected ways long after the original architect's involvement has ceased (Melhuish 2006). Scholars such as Michel Callon (Callon 1996) and more recently Albena Yaneva (Yaneva 2009) have promoted a 'pragmatist', as opposed to 'critical', approach to understanding architectural design, emphasizing the multiple sequences of events and interactions within architectural offices which lead to the emergence of a design proposition and eventually its built realization. Much of this work on architecture from outside architectural theory and practice itself is also associated with a re-framing of buildings primarily as social and technical 'events', rather

◉ understanding of the reality of architectural practice and construction
Detailed section of Infanta Leonor Hospital that shows its consistency with the user-friendly approach

#LVA it's been a pleasure to meet, work with and be a client of LVA. Easy approach, understanding and solution of projects makes you special

MARÍA ARBOLEDAS

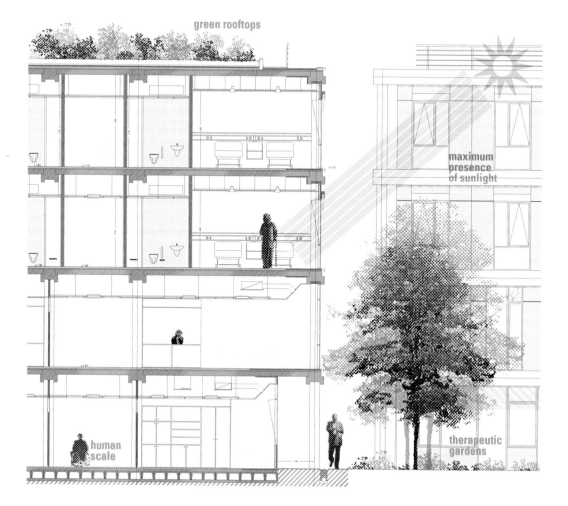

green rooftops

maximum presence of sunlight

human scale

therapeutic gardens

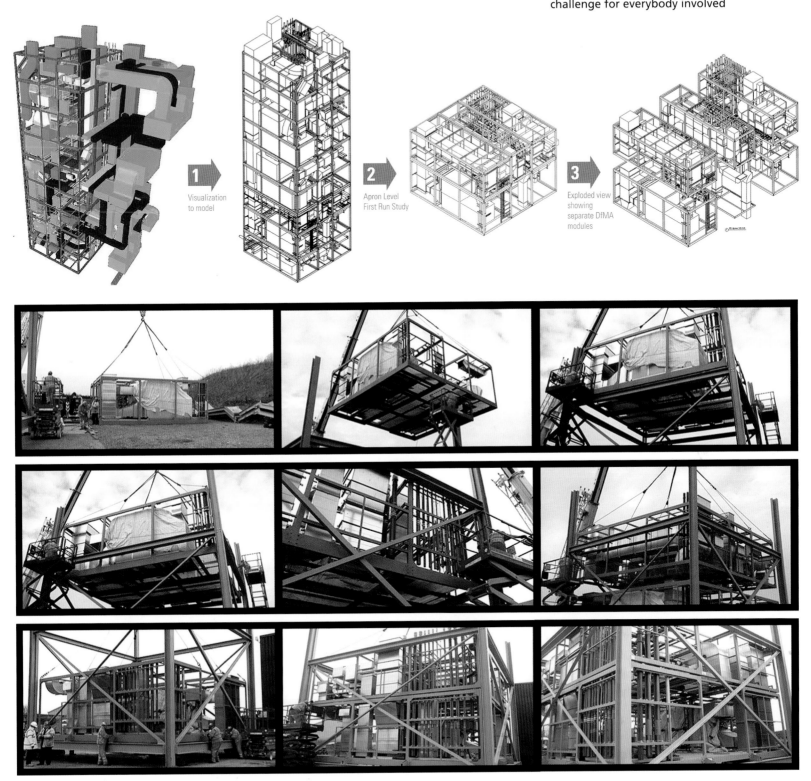

The design of the risers for T2A and their assembly on site has been an enormous challenge for everybody involved

1 Visualization to model

2 Apron Level First Run Study

3 Exploded view showing separate DfMA modules

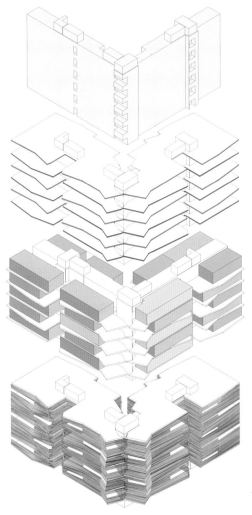

⬆ Axonometry of the components of an apartment building, treated as layers

⬅ The six ward blocks of Vigo Hospital will be painted with prismatic paint, to integrate the buildings in the landscape further

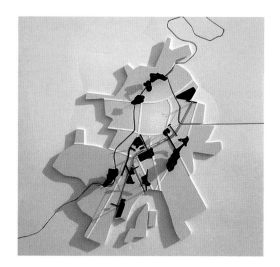

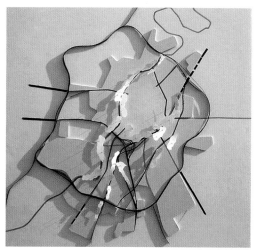

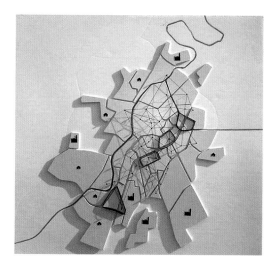

than as architectural typologies, formal compositions or symbolic statements, and it challenges the validity of the traditional bases for evaluating architectural design, as well as the shallow manipulation of architecture to produce icons for aspirational urban brands competing in the cut-throat global market for corporate investment. Vidal's own appraisal of his practice's work represents an acknowledgement of this reality which is comparatively rare, and for that very reason demands critical attention, as well as the respect of his team. 'We don't design a building thinking it's going to be iconic,' he has observed: 'it comes out in the evolution of the building – you don't really know until the end.' What then might be the starting point for design, and the ultimate goal? In the case of Barajas, it was 'no more than a flight schedule', as recalled by Richard Rogers and Simon Smithson – and the aim of making the best possible airport, rather than a vision of an iconic new gateway to Madrid. In the case of Vidal's student project for

City Airport in London, it was as simple as extending the length of the runway to accommodate bigger planes – combined with a more unusual proposition, oxygen-replenishment stations in the concourse for oxygen-deprived frequent flyers. For the Infanta Leonor Hospital at Vallecas, it was to provide facilities for a growing population in the Madrid outskirts. At Vidal's own house in Madrid, it was to create an interesting space for his sons to grow up in and enjoy with friends and family. It is an outlook that involves pragmatism combined with invention, pleasure with problem-solving, and psychology with architecture – an appreciation of the impact of buildings on the lives and experience of their human occupants, an awareness of social issues, and an adaptability to different circumstances. Essentially, it embodies an understanding of the nature of the co-existence of the 'inspiring within the useful' (LV), as opposed to a pursuit of beauty for its own sake.

⬆ starting point
Studies of green corridors, roads and life nodes as starting points for the design of the Valladolid masterplan
➔ see pages 148–151

#ENJOY our three sons, Javier, Pablo and Marc, are always cheerful, open and friendly LUIS VIDAL

⬆ the aim of making the best possible airport
One of Vidal's contributions to Barajas T4, opposed by his partners at the time, was the colour scheme: red-South-hot, blue-North-cold

⬇ enjoy
Luis at home with his three sons

⬇ inspiring within the useful
In the La Marina masterplan, an amazing park is created in an underused pine forest

→ see pages 152–155

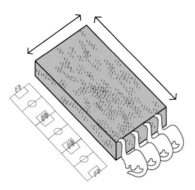

→ bigness
LVA always starts design with a scale study and a context study

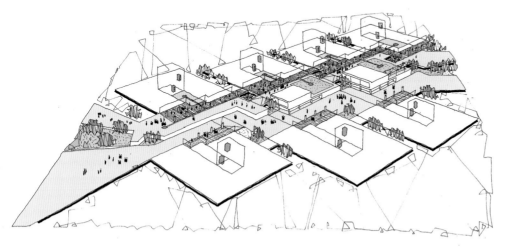

↑ urban life
The CPA office complex acknowledges social interaction in external spaces, so typical of Spain in general and Andalucía in particular
→ see pages 172–177

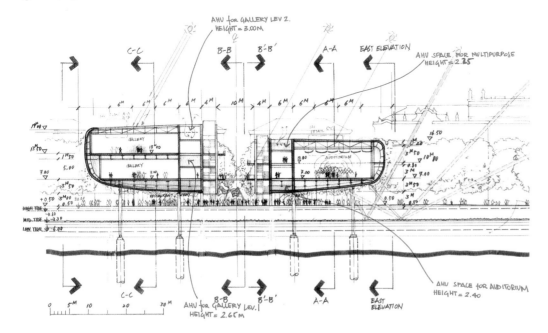

SCALE AND 'BIGNESS': ARCHITECTURE AS SOCIAL EVENT

Working at a very large architectural scale, however, brings with it particular challenges.

Rem Koolhaas has suggested that scale and 'bigness' in buildings means that they 'enter an amoral domain' – where 'their impact is independent of their quality' (OMA/Mau 1995: 501). He proposes that 'a Big Building can no longer be controlled by a single architectural gesture – or any combination of them' and that ultimately, 'All these breaks [associated with bigness] – with scale, with architectural composition, with tradition, with transparency, with ethics – imply the final, most radical break: bigness is no longer part of any urban tissue' (ibid: 502). But LVA's architecture embraces scale while also vigorously engaging with urban tissue and the urban life it hosts; this is the very basis of its moral agenda as a 'service to the public' (LV), and lies at the heart of the way its impact as built intervention is managed. It defines the boundaries between buildings, context and landscape differently, challenging presumptions about where one ends and the other begins, as a connected sequence of events. Architecture then is viewed as 'more than architecture – part of developing society and enjoying social life' (LV). It is a manifestation of social activities and practices, such that transport and infrastructure hubs become great public spaces where people come

← enjoying social life
The Botín Centre building provides sheltered public space underneath it, perfect for the rainy Santander weather
→ see pages 194–197

↑ travelling
Office trip to Peñafiel, with its impressive castle and a main square that doubles as a bull ring

↓ generation of space by means of interaction
External auditorium in Seville's CPA
→ see pages 172–177

together and interact, and architectural references include 'everything we drink, eat, see, every day… We store memories and impressions on personal hard disks in the brain' (LV). Vidal's trips with architectural students from the University of Madrid to different cities were undertaken not so much to visit buildings by other architects as to take in 'the light, the proportions of the streets, the street life, the smell – an instinct which is an anterior perception, which can change your state of mind in a second… You learn architecture by travelling' (LV). It is an approach that is not fundamentally driven or validated by narratives of architectural history and genealogy, but engages with the changing nature of cities, experienced less as clearly defined morphological forms, and rather as messy, elusive, sociotechnical systems – constructed out of physical activities, and enacted into being through complicated networks of people and things interacting together (Farias 2010). In this context, the historic monumental, symbolic and typological character of architecture dissolves into 'a relation of extension between events' and a 'generation of space by means of interaction' (Parisi 2009), with the emphasis on architecture's dynamic human and social dimensions. But, at the same time, it is well understood by LVA that the quality of architecture remains central, because it changes the experience of social interaction wherever it occurs.

Following the theory of airport-hospitals, LVA's big buildings, then, are designed from an open-ended design perspective as interventions that channel and enhance social activity, interaction and event within a specific

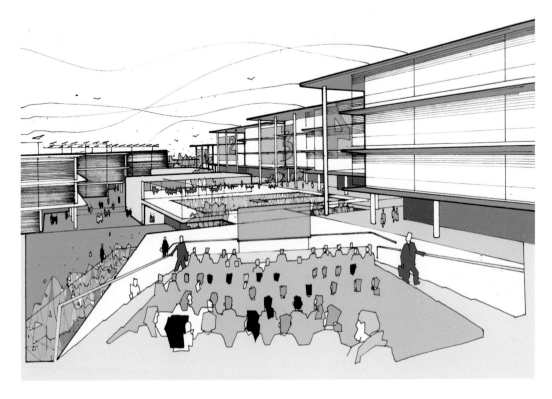

→ → Zaragoza Airport terminal seen from landside

Luis Vidal has an ability rare among architects to exchange ideas in an easy-going and friendly manner

RICHARD ROGERS

◐ ⬆ A normal working day at the shared offices of LVA / RSHP

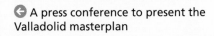

Design review with Richard Rogers in Madrid

Luis Vidal and Richard Rogers

A press conference to present the Valladolid masterplan

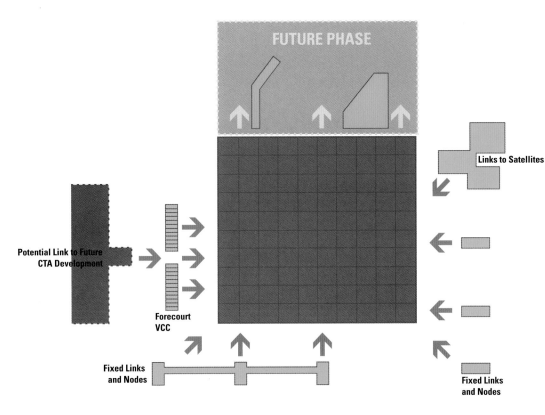

FUTURE PHASE

Links to Satellites

Potential Link to Future
CTA Development

Forecourt
VCC

Fixed Links
and Nodes

Fixed Links
and Nodes

⊝ extension
T2A main building allows for change
and growth without compromising its
strong image

⊙ Buildings grow either by extension
or by addition

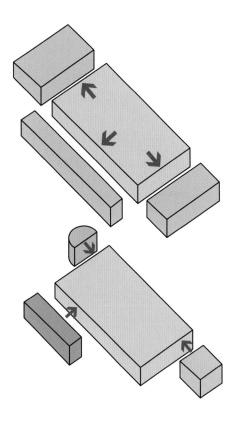

context in the larger sociotechnical framework of the city and city life. They are characterized not only by their large dimensions but also by a complex adaptation to site and landscape, which involves both absorbing and integrating existing routes and circulation patterns into the building framework, providing for their extension in various directions, mapping out trajectories and connections within and beyond a site, and creating landmarks along the way that may be as small as a doorhandle. In contrast to Koolhaas's provocative suggestion that 'its subtext is "f*** context"' (ibid: 502), 'bigness' in LVA's work may be seen as *becoming* context, defined as site and landscape plus social activity, absorbing the detail as well as the larger picture. Buildings are understood and read as organizational systems that maximize the efficiency and integration of spaces within linked volumes which delineate a built topography in themselves, structured by and structuring parallel and sequential spatial practices, and extending the tracks and patterns of movement which already exist around them. But it is the micro-detail within these systems which provides a field of visual and tactile markers – cognitive signifiers – that mediate between people, their actions and the grand scale of the built intervention. So patterns of behaviour in a particular environment are informed by material artefacts and physical qualities, including colour, which give shape and meaning to personal experience, marking thresholds and boundaries, transitions between contrasting areas of activity, within a much larger context.

This may be understood as a process of 'boundary work' or 'integration/ segmentation', through the medium of material markers, which help people to make sense of spatial situations in which they find themselves (Nippert-Eng 1996). It also relates to phenomenological studies of landscape and material culture (e.g. Tilley 1994), which emphasize how real landscapes are read or navigated by people through their bodily movements, senses and interactions with a range of different markers, in contrast to the abstracted and purely visual experience of landscape representation in art.

⬆ colour
Colour-coding aids orientation in an institution as big as Infanta Leonor Hospital

⬇ material markers
Design of a parking-management system for COSIENSA; elements are easily recognizable, with a strong personality and primary focus in user experience

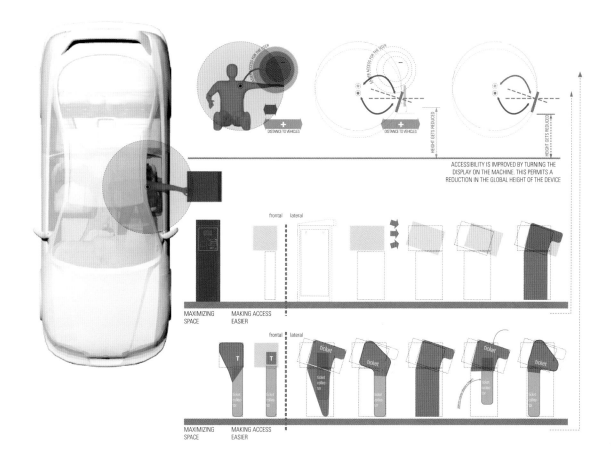

CIRCULATION, FLOW AND PERMEABILITY: FUSION OF THE TECHNICAL AND SOCIAL

As a student in London, Vidal was exposed to Space Syntax theory; its influence as a tool for analyzing circulation, flow and spatial integration, in order to understand the social occupation of space and urban morphologies, may be traced in LVA's work. But Vidal emphasizes that, if it plays a role in the office's work practices, it is rather as an intuitive, common-sense basis for an extended analysis of brief, site and city context, involving many studies and extensive interaction with the client, rather than as a concrete tool. An understanding of circulation and flow through space is central to LVA's projects; flow is essential to airport design, generating a modular approach which also allows for the possibility of future expansion, but it has also permeated the design of other building types in the office – notably

hospitals – in a way that distinguishes the work from that of other architectural practices. However, the interpretation of spatial use and movement grows out of the exploration of brief and site through an organic and collaborative process of dialogue and sketching out of ideas by the project team, rather than a methodical application of Space Syntax theory. It is a programmatic, but also an essentially evolutive approach to design, shaped by a gradual replication, modification and extension of cells or components through which the building's external form and envelope eventually emerges as the outward manifestation of a project's internal DNA. In a sense, then, it is an intuitive interpretation of an analytical approach which brings together the Spanish and Anglo-Saxon ways of making architecture, and never loses sight of the small-scale sensory articulation of the grand overall schema: the 'airport-hospital/hospital-airport' model.

⊙ site
In order to get to grips with Valladolid, the LVA / RSHP team spent almost six months analyzing every aspect of the site and the city
⊙ see pages 148–151

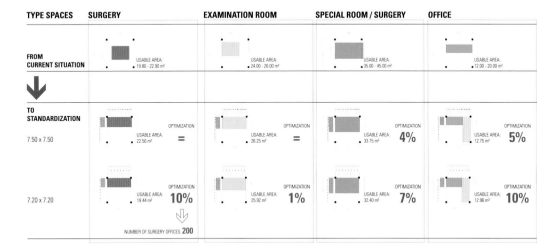

⬆ analysis of brief
LVA studies the brief and improves it with the help of the client

I remember my time working in Spain with RSHP and LVA with great fondness; one of the most rewarding and enjoyable experiences of my professional life

CHRIS DAWSON

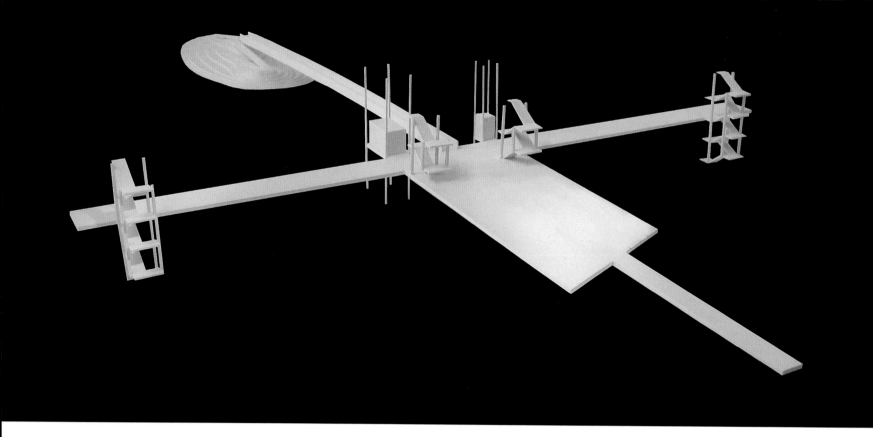

From a conventional perspective, this confusion or merging of distinct architectural typologies undermines the ground rules of architectural design; and yet, viewed from the perspective delineated above, it makes logical sense. As a model, its defining characteristic is identified as a linear and sequential formal strategy comprising chains of segmented volumes, connected by paths of circulation and promenade that can be extended as required and in response to future need and growth. It is non-hierarchical, incremental and topographical, as opposed to monumental, symbolic and symmetrical. There is a strong idea of the building as a performance or event in itself, marshalling a mass of technological information in conjunction with a choreography of different actions and activities along multi-oriented, flexible axes. It is an approach that comes out of LVA's 'passion for functional

architecture', characterized by 'purity of forms and flexible and sustainable solutions' emerging from the 'deep analysis of the objectives and aspirations of our clients' (LVA's curriculum vitae). So, although the challenge of designing hospitals and airports invites the evocation of a technological image in response to the functional precision and technical specification of such projects, the human dimension is strongly present in the development of a hybrid model based on a fusion of the technical and social.

The airport-hospital model provides an interesting case study through which to examine the notion of buildings as permeable, rather than bounded architectural objects, which is pertinent to the discussion of bigness and the problem of scale. 'The permeability of a building... defines the way in which actors pass from one space to another and the way in which boundaries are

⊕ sustainable solutions
LVA's incursions into the media always stress the importance of the environmental, economic and social sustainability of their projects

◀ paths of circulation
Working model of the paths inside the Botín Centre building

↑ ➔ permeable
Different orientations and different louvre arrangements in CPA

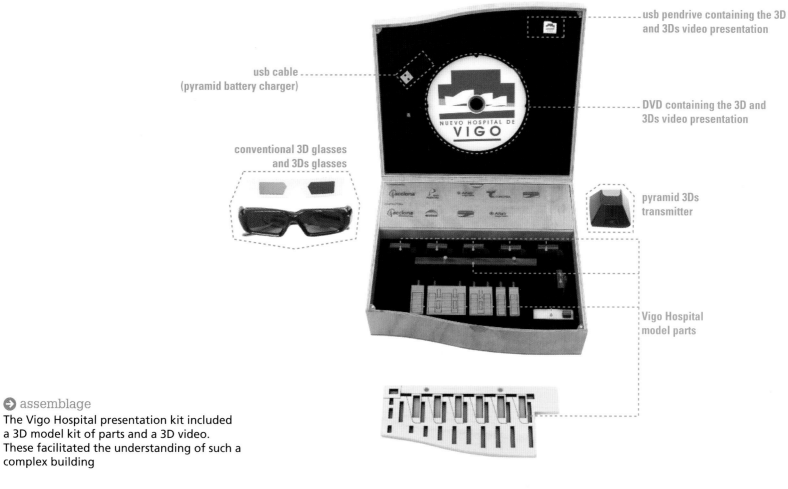

usb pendrive containing the 3D and 3Ds video presentation

usb cable (pyramid battery charger)

DVD containing the 3D and 3Ds video presentation

conventional 3D glasses and 3Ds glasses

pyramid 3Ds transmitter

Vigo Hospital model parts

➔ assemblage

The Vigo Hospital presentation kit included a 3D model kit of parts and a 3D video. These facilitated the understanding of such a complex building

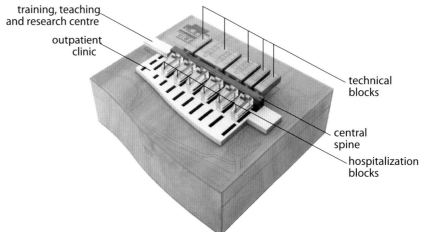

training, teaching and research centre

outpatient clinic

technical blocks

central spine

hospitalization blocks

communicative, intrepid and intelligent, Luis is an example of perseverance that surprises me on a daily basis JUGATX LÓPEZ

constructed' (Jenkins 2002: 223); and thinking about big buildings from this perspective offers a counterpoint to the approach of standard architectural histories to individual buildings as self-contained entities informed by a particular urban, cultural and social context – or cultural artefacts distributed in the landscape, or buildings understood as representative of certain types (ibid: 224). In these accounts, the material definition of a building, specifically its façade, becomes all-important, and an assumption of material stability and fixity becomes fundamental to the understanding of the architectural expression which it embodies. But when a building is considered from the point of view of the user, or actor, or individual moving through space, and engaging in different social scenarios, these criteria become mutable. Stewart Brand has outlined the ways in which people engage with a single place through a number of material and technological levels – including site, structure, skin, services, space plan (interior layout) and stuff (furnishings and fittings) – which may change over time at different rates, and involve different social relationships or networks (Brand 1995). So a building is not just a building, or a work of architecture, or a unified place, but a complicated assemblage of different elements which connect to other different elements in the world beyond.

➔ moving through space
Main pedestrian routes in Valladolid, following streets and crossing squares and parks, and becoming nodes of city life

➔ ➔ Internal image of T2A. Daylight from the north floods the commercial area of the departures hall

	PEDESTRIAN ROUTES
1	PLAZA DE PONIENTE
2	PLAZA MAYOR
3	PLAZA ZORRILLA
4	PLAZA COLÓN
5	NUEVA PLAZA PÚBLICA
6	NUEVA PLAZA LOCAL
7	NUEVA PLAZA LOCAL
8	CUARTELES
9	CONEXIÓN VERDE CON PARQUES METROPOLITANO SUR
10	ARCO DE LADRILLO
11	ARIZA

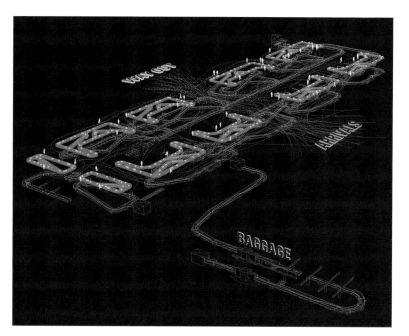

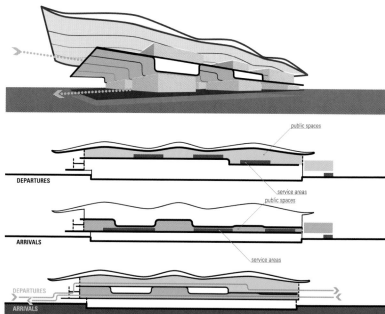

⬆ complexity
The baggage-handling system takes a whole floor under T2A

⬆ terminal building
In T2A the roof is directional and there is a sequence of higher–lower spaces that help flow and orientation in the terminal building. Conceptual sketches from 2008

BUILDINGS AS ASSEMBLAGE

LVA's work acknowledges this complexity in the assemblage, evolution and life of a building, its permeability to the outside world, rather than subscribing to the notion of a finite architectural gesture controlling the entire building project to conform to an image preconceived by the architect. The airport-hospital model exemplifies this complexity and permeability – in terms of bringing together and channelling an array of people, services, technologies, spaces for different activities and the physical boundaries between them. Vidal has described architects as 'adventurers' who have to 'generate a path through life... choosing... discovering things... learning... with an ambition to evolve', and this outlook is in many ways manifested in the office's design approach: 'In order to

be a useful person to society you have to have an ability to adapt to different circumstances.' Playing a key role in designing and delivering the airport terminal at Barajas, at the age of 28, with the Richard Rogers Partnership, was 'a great adventure', which can also be seen as a manifesto for the office's subsequent work. Although the design's most immediate visual impact might be identified as the unusual rainbow-coloured parade of columns (see page 49) extending from the south (red) to the north (blue, passing through yellow) end of the terminal building, its outstanding feature is the sense of both vertical and horizontal connection and permeability: a strong sense of sequential progression or flow into, through and out of the building from one side to the other, and from bottom to top through successive layers. The terminal was conceived as a

series of separately articulated buildings connected by bridges across open wells. On landside, car-parking in six 'bins', or pods, feeds in to check-in and security ('processing'), which lead to departures in a long transverse pier, interpolated by departure gates along its length on airside, and the runways themselves. Below is the arrivals floor, and beneath that, the concourse to the new metro station, connected to each other and the floor above by open escalators, a little reminiscent of the Pompidou Centre. Travellers and their associates pass from one point to the next, while enjoying clear views through the building along a number of axes, and a wealth of natural light through its permeable, glazed envelope, which is combined with indirect artificial lighting reflected off the underside of the roof. It is calm and spacious inside, acoustically muted,

⬆ ⬇ natural light

Zaragoza terminal's roof was designed to provide the best natural light to the main waiting areas furthest from the façades

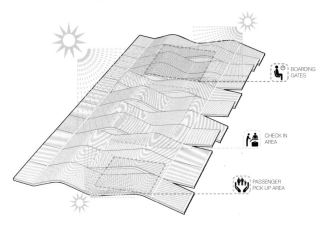

BOARDING GATES

CHECK IN AREA

PASSENGER PICK UP AREA

⬆ pier

Unlike T4 at Barajas, T2A has no pier as such. FLANs (Fixed Links and Nodes) connect the building with the aeroplanes

PIER 218
PIER 218
PIER 219-2
PIER 225-226
PIER 224
PIER 223

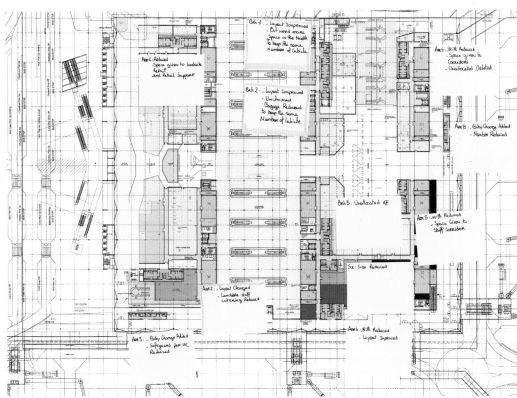

Infanta Leonor Hospital, also known within LVA as Vallecas Hospital

analyzing functional problems and proposing solutions
LVA's notes taken at a T2A fine-tuning meeting during the Programme A phase of works

the floors designed with a matt finish to maintain the atmosphere of calm.

Barajas was conceived at competition stage to reduce the distances passengers have to walk, by linking arrival, check-in, security and boarding along specific routes designated according to which plane a passenger is travelling on. Unfortunately, the higher cost of staffing multiple security check-points, and the diffusion of retail outlets across a wider area led to the installation of one central security point instead, so all passengers have to pass through the centre and then out again, and end up walking much more. But the long pier design of the departures building allows planes to approach from both sides, accommodating higher

levels of air traffic. These strategic planning considerations are driven by a relish for analyzing functional problems and proposing solutions, based on the fundamental principle that 'airports have to be flexible, they always change and they always grow'. Yet this approach is at the same time combined with an investment of attention to the details of flooring, lighting and colour throughout the building, the spatial and sensory detail at local level as it is experienced by people navigating a route from one point to the next, which manifests a commitment to the quality of services and 'stuff' (in Brand's words) within the overall structure.

#ZARAGOZA **I wish airports retained a human scale more often. Although flexibility of growth was carefully solved, I truly hope the expansion never takes place** BÁRBARA PÉREZ

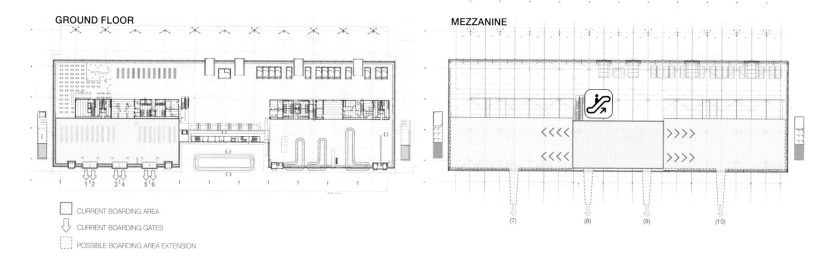

GROUND FLOOR

MEZZANINE

☐ CURRENT BOARDING AREA

⇩ CURRENT BOARDING GATES

⬚ POSSIBLE BOARDING AREA EXTENSION

Zaragoza, the 'little brother' of Barajas, channels 750,000 passengers per annum, but was designed with inbuilt flexibility which would allow it to expand to accommodate 2.5 million if necessary: 'thinking flexibly, we built this mezzanine level at the right place and height so that it could become a departures lounge in the future, with fingers straight into the planes' (LV). It is a classical one-level terminal with departures and arrivals at ground level, and remote gates within walking distance; but the top floor was designed and constructed so that it could become a pier in future, with departures accommodated on a 'finger' at the upper level with air bridges added to it, and

lateral extensions on both sides. It replaces an old terminal (still standing), which was considered unsuitable as a 'doorway to a world Expo' (LV). On the other side of it is a busy existing cargo terminal, which is the hub for the fashion retailer Zara's export operation worldwide, as well as a big local market for fresh fish and a large supermarket chain, making it the third largest cargo terminal in Spain.

The new passenger terminal was low-cost but designed with 'grand' elements that would provide an inspiring welcome to visitors to the Zaragoza Expo. A beautiful green granite floor, verdecotto from Brazil, was inspired by the texture of sand when the tide goes out, relating

⬆ mezzanine level
Diagrams showing current boarding area on the ground floor and a proposed one on a mezzanine level, for future expansion of Zaragoza Airport terminal

← waves hitting the beach
The roof 'goes crazy' on the landside
of the building

↓ flat on airside
The roof is flat at the airside end

to the characteristic design of the roof in 'waves' – completely flat on airside, like the calm in the middle of the sea, then, on landside, waves hitting the beach, breaking in sequence on the sand. 'I'm a sailor, that's my dream profession, that's one of my passions in life,' comments Vidal, but it is an enthusiasm for all modes of travel and connection that underlies the work. The green granite surface runs out of the building to the front, where it is honed so people do not slip when it is wet, and, inside, up against the wall separating landside and airside. Overhead, the underside of the Kalzip roof is exposed, without a soffit, and illuminated by a combination of natural light through rooflights

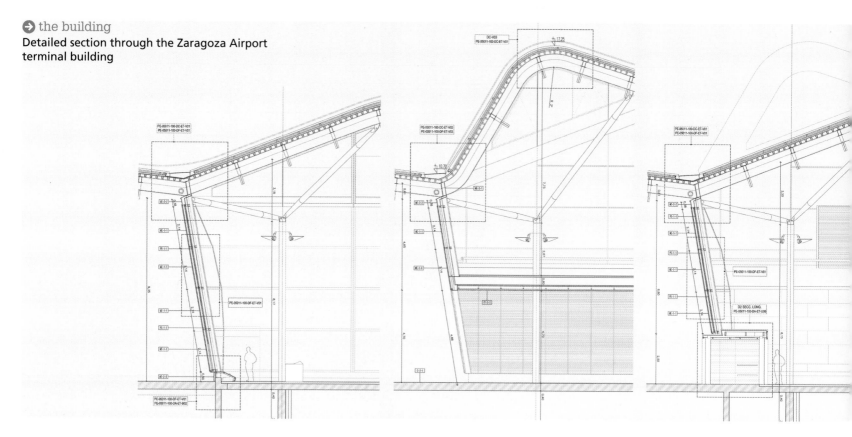

'between the waves', and uplighting which 'shoots light onto the coffer' from lamps mounted on the tall structural 'trees' which are supporting the roof. The light reflection is enhanced by the dark copper-coloured paint finish to the roof, which is also intended to provide a level of 'comfort' and 'extra kindness' to passengers that would not be achieved with a bright, shiny metallic finish.

As at Barajas, but on a much smaller scale, there is a sense of calm order and progression in the way the terminal is assembled, which starts at the car-parking stands outside, and progresses via a series of thresholds through the building to the planes in their stands on airside, and back again in reverse direction. At the same time, the building functions not only as a place of transit, or a place of smooth-running technical operation, but also as a site of sociability, interaction and exchange which is

responsive to the way in which it is used. As Vidal explains, international airports were 'so dark, dull' when he was a student in London, and he was 'always interested in public buildings that can treat the user in a better way' (LV) – as an extension of urban, social activity. The old terminal at Zaragoza, for example, had a restaurant 'that was always packed with local people, lots of people used to come here for lunch, and you walked up there and saw the planes on the airside – it had an amazing atmosphere' (LV). Designed by a local engineering firm, it did not have the architectural prestige demanded by the Expo, but it was alive and integrated with local city life. The new terminal, with its large, bright, busy café at one end, filled with tables and chairs designed by LVA, its children's play area, and rentable on-site conference facilities, has this quality too; and, with provision

for a new restaurant on the upper level, it is explicitly designed to continue to grow in sociability in the future, as well as in physical size and quantity of air traffic.

Just as Zaragoza gently channels flows of people in and out, carefully demarcating between landside and airside, national and international, travellers and those who come just to interact, the hospitals of Vallecas (Infanta Leonor) and Ibiza (Can Misses) also bring together and channel an array of people, services, technologies and spaces for different activities within an overall architectural schema characterized by scale rather than an immediately recognizable style. Zaragoza constitutes a distinct 'gateway' to the city, but Infanta Leonor and Can Misses create an extension of the landscape which surrounds them into built form where flows of staff and

LVA: since 2004, architecture in motion with its own philosophy and a unique formula ISABEL PASCUAL

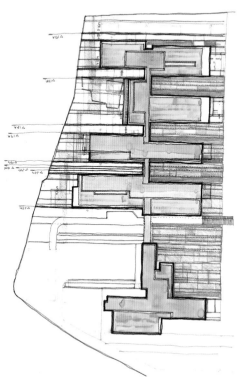

↑ landscape
Initial ideas for landscaping at Can Misses

← church tower

Two of the Infanta Leonor Hospital satellites seen from the central spine, with the historic centre of Vallecas in the background

↓ vertical connections

Aerial view of Can Misses, with Ibiza Bay in the distance

→ see pages 182–187

↓ → Infanta Leonor Hospital in the Vallecas district of Madrid

→ see pages 178–181

'passengers' or 'passing users' meet at different points before moving on. The modular logic is punctuated by gestures of recognition of the outside world – a vista along an axis focused on a church tower in the distance, multiple points of ingress and egress, a colour scheme (red, orange, blue) evoking sunset on the sea – rather than determined by any single monumental entrance, or search for 'a brand look'.

Evoking the traditional concepts of building, city, landscape, one of the orange-coded architects (see page 115) in the Can Misses Hospital team comments that 'A hospital is like a little city' in itself. Yet at the same time, she identifies the five common elements in diagrammatic and relational terms which do not reference a visual image of the city, but rather the framework of nodes, links and flows which make it work. So the building works at two scales – the overall image or schema of the 'city', understood as a network of flows and segregated/integrated spaces which are coded by colour; and the micro-neighbourhoods within it (wards in four-storey blocks, and functional amenities in two-storey blocks), all of which are subsumed into the larger scale of the city of Ibiza and the seaboard, through its lines and borders – main roads – which connect into the existing landscape of streets and urban fabric around it. But within this concept, the segregation and coming together of 'processed' and 'unprocessed' staff, patients and visitors, again just as in the airport schemes, is fundamental. The colour-coding scheme underpins this rigorous structure, with white and blue used for the exterior, following traditional custom (blue is thought to kill insects, and perceived as a 'healthy' colour); blue again for thresholds and vertical connections (stairs and lifts); blue doors and orange walkways for external people; white doors and walkways for internal people; and red control points.

Similarly, the Infanta Leonor Hospital at Vallecas, in Madrid, is clearly structured by a concept of segregation, integration and flow, represented by a colour scheme which has produced a graphic now worn as a badge by hospital staff. Unlike Can Misses, Infanta Leonor was not designed to grow in future, but rather to over-provide space that can be filled in due course according to requirements. Also in contrast to Can Misses, the landscape immediately surrounding the site was a blank canvas, and the main access to the hospital was relocated during the course of the project. Thus, in a sense, the immediate physical context is fluid, while at the same time the connection with the larger urban landscape is spelled out through the orientation and modulation of the building, and the social and environmental context is very clear.

The Vallecas model stood out at the time it was commissioned as one of seven new hospitals for Madrid. It offers a strong sense of linear promenade through segregated blocks keyed in to a central spine in which the main inpatient arrival point is situated. But there are other entrances to the hospital too – the A&E arrival point and the outpatient entrance – and there is no clear architectural hierarchy between the different entrance façades of the building. Each block is colour-coded on the exterior, to distinguish its function from its neighbours, and the spaces in between are filled with gardens designed to withstand the strong Madrid sun. The fragmentation of the standard deep-plan volume of modern hospital typology makes for a naturally well-lit interior, and allows views out across the landscape from many different vantage points which underline the connection between the internal life of the hospital and the physical and social worlds that lie beyond, and to which its occupants will return at the end of their visit or working shift. Circulation routes within the interior are clearly segregated between staff, patients and visitors, allowing for a complex network of flows within a reduced overall surface area, which impressed the client.

ARCHITECTURAL AESTHETICS AND IDENTITY

The sense of buildings designed as extensions between different events occurring in different spaces, or 'movement in extension' as Luciana Parisi puts it (Parisi 2009), is strong in the buildings that come out of the LVA office. It is, if you like, a process of 'heterogeneous engineering' which brings many different elements together, reflecting the idea of architects as 'engineer-sociologists' discussed by David Brain (Brain 1994), and buildings as framed activity, which have to be enacted into being. Brain describes the modernist reconstruction of design practice, specifically in the field of public housing, as an example of how practical

#HOSPITAL when somebody really understands patients and designs a space *for* them, that person helps them heal faster

JUAN LÓPEZ-IBOR

◀ colour-coded on the exterior
Both colour and fragmentation of volume help break up the otherwise imposing length of the Infanta Leonor Hospital

↑ framed activity
When one sees the fit-out plan of the hospital, it is easy to imagine it full of users and activity

01 TETRA BRIKS
* Recycled cardboard   * Maplar   * Teclan

02 WOOD
* Chipboard: : panels, floors, roofs, enclosure : formwork
* Thermal insulation
* Fuel: ashes destined for agricultural purposes

03 PLASTIC
* Recycled plastic and vegetable fibre panels   * Recycled plastic panels - Insulation

04 TYRES
* Battens. Retaining walls
* Floorings
* Soundproofing. Noise and impact

05 PAPER/CARDBOARD
* Recycled paper panels   * Paper bricks "Papercrete"

⬆ social technology
Study of possibilities for recycling garbage to make construction materials, applied to South American countries

⬇ a mix of sensory qualities
Valladolid masterplan image showing how the public space in front of the new transportation hub could look and feel

expertise and theoretical discourse become inscribed in buildings as a particular social technology. But where then does this leave the question of architectural aesthetics and identity?

Koolhaas, in his discourse on 'bigness' in buildings, criticized the Pompidou Centre in Paris as an exemplar of High-Tech architectural ideology, for proposing 'spaces where "anything" [i.e. events, activities] was possible', constituting a level of flexibility which 'led to *entity* at the price of *identity*'. Scale, flexibility and an affiliation with the High-Tech aesthetic, born of a love of complex projects and sophisticated engineered solutions, also characterize the work of the Vidal office. Luis Vidal speaks more of sociological and technological change, and the importance of technical innovation as 'added value', than of architectural aesthetics. As he says, the office is 'very open-minded about structures and techniques', and pragmatic about the decisions that have to be made in order to create strong co-operative alliances with clients. Architecture is viewed as a process that leads to results, characterized by a mix of sensory qualities including 'orientation, flexibility, texture and colours' rather than clearly defined visual criteria, and not as a predetermined goal. Yet at the same time, Vidal is clear that the importance of the new generation of airports which came out of the offices of Rogers, Foster, Piano – Heathrow T5, Stansted, Kansai – and now his own, is also embodied as much in their role as 'gateways' to cities, celebrating travel, as opposed to the basic processing plants which they had been. And, from his point of view, the Pompidou is most significant for the great public space in front of it, where people come together and interact: 'Everyone thinks Pompidou

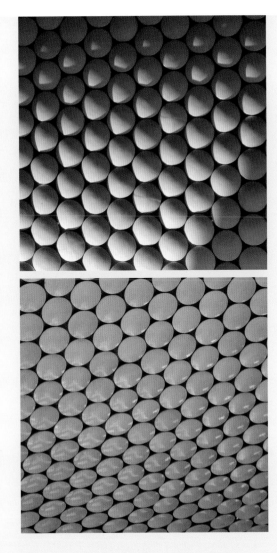

⬆ The curved building envelope of the Botín Centre is formed of ceramic buttons that reveal a changing image in different light conditions or at different times of the day

➡ Mock-up of the Botín Centre façade

if this is the century of teams, it will be LVA's. We've never seen such a group of talents so closely knit, while at the same time including the client

JOAQUÍN AND MAVÍ IBÁÑEZ

⊙ identity in the city
In LVA / RPBW's proposal, the intended site of the Botín Centre was changed to align with a pedestrian axis in Santander

is just an art centre – but they're wrong. Its identity in the city is the piazza in front of the building' (LV 12.11).

In contrast to some of these practices, Vidal's office promotes 'no particular image for architecture', as one staff member puts it, and no parameters or limits are set on the formal possibilities which the team might develop. This conception of the symbolic and social role of buildings embedded in their processual and technical logic implicates the production of recognizable architectural aesthetics and visual identity as part of the design process. The projects for Zaragoza and Heathrow Terminal 2A demonstrate how an engineered, sociotechnical solution can achieve this sense of identity, and avoid becoming mere architectural 'entity', through the creation of a distinct sense of place through social interaction, which is evocative of Paul Andreu's view, eloquently expressed: 'Terminals have become more important these days than cultural spaces such as

museums or theatres where societies used to assemble... their space... is the locus of meeting between what is most universal, mobile and modern – the aeroplane, that dangerous marvel – and what is most primitive – the sense of belonging to a place and the very deep-seated desire to fly to be somewhere else at once' (Andreu, in Binney 1999).

Vidal's team emphasize the driving force behind the work as one of 'being logical', rather than pursuing 'a shape, or a look'. As one blue-coded architect (see page 115) says, they 'have no fear of showing things the way they are', rather than concealing the technical and structural content of buildings behind an aesthetic veneer. Vidal himself has commented, 'I don't like the word beautiful'. Part of the problem with buildings which have a very clearly defined, fixed aesthetic, or which consciously strive after a conception of 'beauty', is that they effectively constrain and limit future change and growth. By contrast, LVA's projects are designed

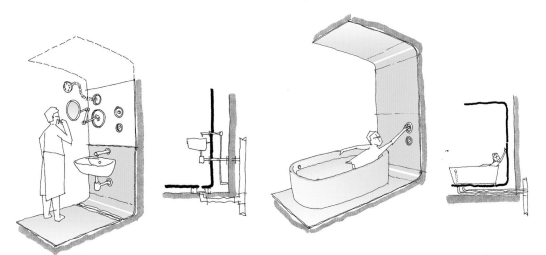

← no parameters or limits
Early sketches of the NOKEN MOOD sanitaryware collection, the aesthetics of which derive from user friendliness and ease of construction

⬇ Heathrow Terminal 2A
The simple gesture of T2A's roof gives a strong identity both from the inside and from the air

↑ identity happens by itself
The carefully planned solar shading of
CPA determines the overall identity
of the buildings

⊕ see pages 172–177

Luis understands that the business side
of architecture provides the finance for
R&D of ideas, and the means to see them
through to completion LENNART GRUT

84 Design as an open-ended process

for change and growth, and 'identity happens by itself', even developing over time, rather than being preconceived. Within this process, the textures and colours which are incorporated within the technical framework of the building, comprising structure, skin, services and 'stuff' inside (to quote Brand), are vital to the generation of that sense of well-being, enjoyment and calm which Vidal sees as fundamental to the purpose of architecture, in contrast to the often-cited 'wow' factor, the spectacular visual gesture, which many clients, notably in China and the Gulf, unthinkingly commission from global practices on the 'starchitect' circuit (Ren 2011; Elsheshtawy 2010).

Vidal describes colour as 'an essential element… it will affect your mood'. The psychological impact of colour, the combination of colours, has always been a key interest; at the same time colour is embraced by the office as a functional mechanism for coding complex buildings visually and making them more legible and easier to navigate, both internally and externally, as elements of a much larger landscape (see Ibiza and Vallecas). In LVA's buildings, colour carries meaning.

Thus colour substantially contributes to the identity of buildings, as places of well-being, of sociability, and as physical gateways or landmarks which contribute to a sense of topographical and cultural place, even where the concept of place may seem to have become an irrelevance compared to the scale of infrastructure and functional accommodation demanded in rapidly urbanizing contexts. As Vidal observes, 7.2 billion people will be living in cities within 50 years (as opposed to 3 billion in 2000), and architects have to work out how to respond to that challenge. However, as the sociologist Saskia Sassen has pointed out (Sassen 2012 [1994]), 'place' in itself has not become obsolete, since new forms of territorial centralization and organization are emerging out of a process of technological and sociological change – a process that Vidal compares in its impact to that of the French and Industrial Revolutions. Buildings will therefore continue to have a role to play in the identification of place, through their own visual and aesthetic identity, which directly relates to the changing conditions of scale, complexity and flexibility within which they are embedded. Although the buildings produced by the Vidal office embrace the infrastructural scale of development and accommodation in the contemporary era, they also therefore, and especially through approaches to colour and texture, respond to the continuing need for buildings to express architectural identity without engaging in a blind pursuit of shape and image.

COLOUR AND TEXTURE

Vidal's approach to colour in his architecture is characterized by the use of the strong primaries and hues – manifested also in the design of the office's colourful business cards – and from that point of view bears some similarities with the work of RSHP. As Rogers comments, the two practices concur on the use of colour to underline certain forms of visual organization, but also, citing the case of Barajas, to create 'a happy place'. Rogers suggests that 'colour is easy in Spain', because, as a result of southern European climate and culture, there is naturally more and stronger colour in the environment than in the northern European countries, which are characterized by muted tones and grey skies. His comments imply a

greater resistance to the use of strong colour in architecture in the UK and other northern European countries, where perhaps there persists an underlying distrust of colour in buildings as somehow brash and vulgar, which is not found in Spain.

But Vidal was also influenced by the work of the Swiss Expressionist painter and theorist Johannes Itten, notably his book *The Art of Colour* (1920), to which Vidal was originally referred by Peter Lee. He cites the direct impact of this book on the decision to use the colours of the rainbow spectrum for the promenade of structural trees at Barajas Airport. Itten underlined the psychological effects of colour, writing that 'colours are radiating forces generating energies which have

↑ colourful business cards
Front and back of some of LVA's business cards

red lipstick sales increase during a recession. LVA picks brighter Pantones for business cards. Cheerful, mighty, upbeat colours

MÓNICA VILLALBA

◀ forces generating energies
An almost neon yellow shouts 'emergency' in CPA's fire staircases

⬇ Itten
Image based on one of Itten's famous colour wheels

intense days of work in Italian, English and Spanish, with only one goal: to give the city of Santander a renovated heart

PATRICIA LOZANO

⬅ View of the Botín Centre from the park in which it sits

➡ see pages 194–197

either a positive or a negative effect on us, whether we realize it or not… the deepest and truest secrets of colour effect are, I know, invisible even to the eye and are beheld by the heart alone. The essential eludes conceptual formulation.' Itten built on a tradition of thinking about colour established by Goethe and Schopenhauer, who forwarded ideas from mystical, philosophical and alchemical sources in opposition to Newton's scientific analysis of colour in *Opticks* (1704) as a refraction of light against particles of matter and onto the eye. Itten contributed to a re-evaluation of colour in twentieth-century avant-garde art and architecture, as a source of human vitality, which Bruno Taut described as a reaction against the livid greyness of the previous century, caused by the pre-eminence of 'thought, which rather than being productive or life-giving robbed its countenance of the glow of health' (Taut 1925; see also Melhuish 1993).

Taut's comments are interesting in light of the dominance in the late twentieth and early twenty-first centuries of concrete, steel and glass as modern construction materials which are well suited to the realization of massive extendable structures and

⬇ source of human vitality
The colour strategy for Can Misses is based on the colours of Ibiza

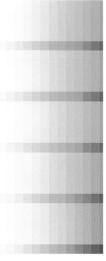

COLOUR: **BLUE**
MEANING: THRESHOLD
CONFIGURATION: SPATIAL / VOLUMETRIC
ELEMENTS: MILESTONES. ENTRANCES /
STAIRS AND ELEVATORS / EXAMINATION
ROOMS AND OFFICES

ENTRANCES

DOORS

STAIRS AND ELEVATORS

EXAMINATION ROOMS/
OFFICES

COLOUR: **ORANGE**
MEANING: ROUTES
CONFIGURATION: LINEAR
ELEMENTS: PATHS / CORRIDORS

CORRIDORS

COLOUR: **RED**
MEANING: WARNING
CONFIGURATION: PUNCTUAL
ELEMENTS: NODES / CONTROL
DESKS

CONTROL DESKS

when we eat together we order a dish we have never tried before. Our collaborations have been in the same spirit – adventures with fun SIMON SMITHSON

⬇ Luis Vidal and Simon Smithson in Valladolid, March 2013

infrastructure, but have also contributed to the increasing '(re-)greyification' of the contemporary built environment and urban/peri-urban landscape. At the same time, the impact of 'colour pollution', caused by indiscriminate advertising, badly thought-out street signage and ill-considered use of the new ranges of coloured materials, especially cladding materials, progressively available to the construction industry, is also considerable.

Colour and materials, textures of surfaces and 'stuff', are of course inextricably linked, and this awareness always informs the approach in the LVA office to designing large-scale, flexible buildings which by necessity must

be constructed in steel or concrete. So colour is embedded in the design agenda, within the framework of 'three orders' defined by Vidal as: the overall container (steel or concrete); secondary elements within it – the 'big chunky things'; and the smaller elements, down to the very smallest, such as signage, lighting and switches, which people engage with at an intimate level as they move around a space. It may take the form of strongly coloured metallic panels from the RAL range, as on the hospitals of Vallecas and Ibiza, where blue is used for its traditional symbolic association with health, but where Vidal also challenged the team to design the bedroom blocks in black; or the already

mentioned painted, rainbow-coloured steel columns at Barajas (from the much bigger German NTC range), moving symbolically from (hot) red in the south, through yellow, to (cooler) blue in the north. But it also encompasses softer and more subtle colours, such as those embodied in the green granite flooring of Zaragoza Airport, also used in the swimming pool of Vidal's own house, the uplit Kalzip soffit, or the fall of sunlight through the rooflights in the undulating roof structure at Zaragoza or Heathrow T2A, which brings the interiors to life with light and shadows, changing the sensory perception of surface and texture throughout the day. As Vidal explains, the formula

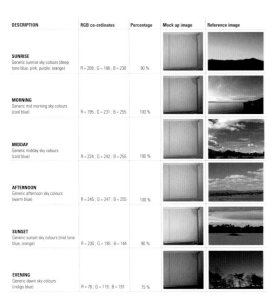

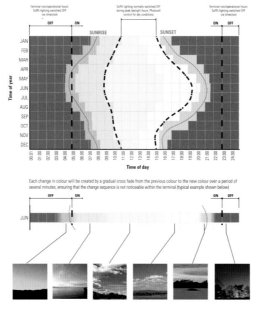

⬅ colour and materials
T2A's soffit incorporates lighting to mimic natural sunlight, which changes with time and weather conditions

⬇ Vallecas
Colour-coding of the façades of Infanta Leonor. Colour saturation subtly increases on the upper floors

URGENCIAS

they aim for is a contrast between the highly charged and the more neutral – a neutral office furnished with brightly coloured chairs, or vice versa – but at the same time there are many gradations in between, generated by the natural, inherent colours of carefully selected and combined materials, which give the spatial environment a sensory and visual depth that is vital to the creation of a distinctive architectural identity, as well as a calm and orderly atmosphere that encourages enjoyment of what can otherwise often be stressful procedures.

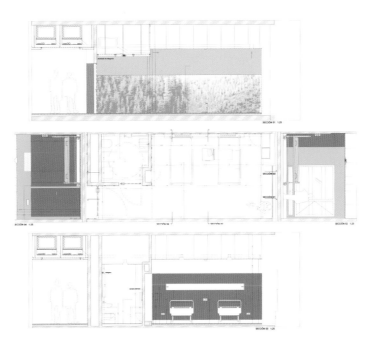

⬆ brings the interiors to life
Green has a calming effect. Typical room in Vigo Hospital

⬅ Zaragoza
The copper colour of the underside of the roof helps the geometry of the rooflights stand out

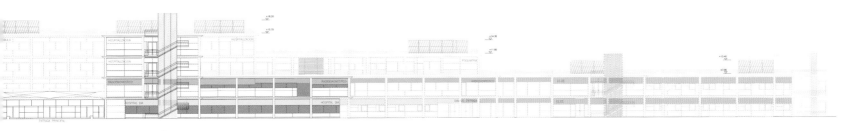

ENVIRONMENTAL RESPONSIBILITY

The LVA team's approach to colour and texture in buildings is highly integrated within a larger framework of environmental responsibility that also plays a key role in defining a particular type of architectural identity within the context of the kind of large-scale, complex projects that have generated the anonymous, un-rooted, technical landscapes defined by the French anthropologist Marc Augé as 'non-places'. Augé defined 'non-places' as characteristic of an era of super-modernity, in which uprootedness is

the norm, and humans cannot recognize themselves in their environment (Augé in Melhuish 1996: 82–83). He suggests that 'today, all of our circulation and information spaces can be considered as non-places. As a rule they do not serve as meeting places.' Vidal's architectural agenda, as already described, is driven by the need to create circulation and information spaces that are specifically conceived as places of social interaction, performance and identity, within and extending beyond buildings, which also carry their own architectural identity in the landscapes created by 'super-modernity'. Architecture is, once again,

⊙ ⊙ circulation
Wide enough to allow for chatting and with ample seating, circulation spaces in CPA are carefully designed and integrated with the spaces they serve

Luis Vidal: tenacity, self-commitment, rigour and ambition are elements that build beyond good architecture and outlive it ANNA GIRÓ

WE MUST REBUILD
THE EMPTY NEIGHBOURHOODS
TO INCREASE
URBAN SUSTAINABILITY
(DENSITY, TRANSPORTATION, CONNECTIVITY,
SECURITY, WEALTH... ETC)

⬆ environmental responsibility
By increasing population density, cities can
afford expensive 'greener' infrastructures

⬇ reduce CO_2 emissions
Sustainability is extremely difficult to quantify.
Independent international associations set
criteria and certify buildings

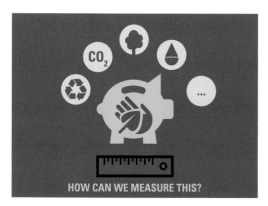

a 'service to the public'. But Vidal is also
adamant that part of this service, under
the conditions of super-modernity, is
a consistent and effective approach to
environmental responsibility, embodied
in architectural design, which, to date,
goes against prevailing trends in Spain.
As he says, part of their work involves
'making clients, cities' representatives
and politicians aware that long-term
environmental responsibility is an
issue we need to address: And, believe
me, we have been preaching a lot!'
(LV 12.11). In turn, well-engineered
environmental solutions play a key
role in the production of a humanized
architecture which can create a sense
of rootedness and belonging in a
sustainable world.

Environmental responsibility is
described as 'the DNA of the studio';
above all, the task of design, through
massing of volumes, treatment of the
façade, and the embracing of innovative
technologies such as the chilled beam,
is to control the penetration of light
into buildings, prevent overheating and
cut energy consumption dramatically.
At Heathrow T2A the aim is to reduce
CO_2 emissions by 40%. Often, clients
are reluctant to invest in sustainability,
but as technology improves, it
becomes easier to prove the case for
its implementation. In the main, Vidal
endorses the use of traditional, also
known as passive, methods of cooling
from 'the time of our grandparents' –
appropriate orientation, thermal mass,
façade shading and cross-ventilation –
to meet the needs of modern buildings
such as offices and retail environments,
which require cooling most of the day
throughout the year because of the heat
generated inside them by machinery
and people.

This includes a preference for the
use of concrete structures rather than

⬇ approach
For CPA, LVA / RSHP followed every one of Arup's guidelines, to ensure that the complex would achieve LEED Platinum certification once finalized

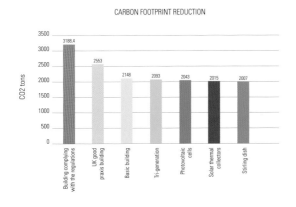

CARBON FOOTPRINT REDUCTION

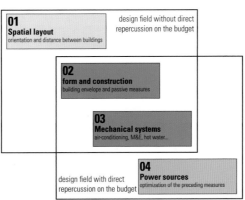

01
Spatial layout
orientation and distance between buildings

design field without direct repercussion on the budget

02
form and construction
building envelope and passive measures

03
Mechanical systems
air-conditioning, M&E, hot water...

04
Power sources
optimization of the preceding measures

design field with direct repercussion on the budget

steel where possible, although, as Vidal stresses, the necessity of designing for flexibility and future growth, through modularity and repetition of elements, renders steel structures better suited especially to airport building. His approach contrasts, then, with some of the large-scale transport structures designed by his fellow architects in Spain, such as Moneo's airport in Seville, a concrete, load-bearing structure described by Antón Capitel as 'a strange palacio which is unexpected in this location' (Capitel in Cuadra 2007: 78). Or, for example, Ferrater's concrete and steel railway station for the high-speed rail link into Zaragoza from Madrid. LVA's buildings follow more closely in the tradition of the functional, extendable and environmentally efficient 'big roof' established by Foster's Stansted, as opposed to the monumental and symbolic 'palacio' model which has been characteristic of much contemporary Spanish architectural production.

On the other hand, the new hospital at Ibiza is a concrete structure, following on from the model established with Vallecas, and leading the way for the new hospital of Vigo in the north of the country. The heavy V-shaped supporting columns rooted in the ground (and echoing the distinctive form of the steel columns used along the façade at Zaragoza) are made in situ and generate an efficient structural solution.

In the hospital models the concept of the big, sheltering and typically undulating roof over-arching a number of defined top- and side-lit volumes is broken down into more complex massing arrangements. Following the pattern of a central spine connecting smaller linked buildings giving shape to different functional zones (clinical, nursing, technical, outpatients, etc.), this strategy also contributes to the

⬆ One of the private offices of CPA

➡ The buildings of CPA in Seville are adapted to the natural variations in ground level

⊙ see pages 172–177

environmental programme. Smaller building masses allow for more effective cross-ventilation, while also generating interstitial outdoor spaces in the form of relatively narrow gardens and patios which offer higher levels of natural light but also contribute to shading of façades. In addition, smaller blocks of varying height allow for the implementation of 'green roofs' where appropriate, as well as an increased number of views out of the buildings, at different angles,

both onto the immediate environment of maintained outdoor spaces, and also onto the wider landscape, contributing to the psychological welfare of patients and staff alike.

Façade shading is one of the key areas of sustainable design, and has been achieved by LVA in various ways, including the use of horizontal or vertical steel 'lamas' or fins across glazed areas of façade, overhangs and other screening devices. These are some of the methods

which LVA has explored across a range of building types, not confined to airports and hospitals, but also including offices, housing and cultural buildings, balancing the desire for natural light with the necessity of controlling solar gain.

For example, the CPA office complex designed in collaboration with RSHP for the multinational Abengoa in Seville set a new standard for environmental efficiency, recognized with a LEED Platinum award and the RIBA Award for

⊙ screening devices
First studies for the T2A south façade, showing a combination of shading systems

⊙ explored
Explanatory drawings showing how the natural ventilation of the FLANs (Fixed Links And Nodes) of T2A could work. 2008 proposal

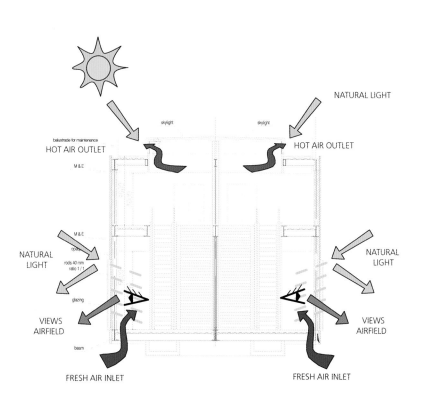

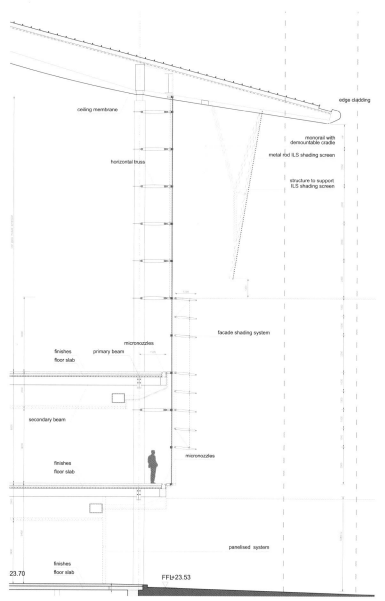

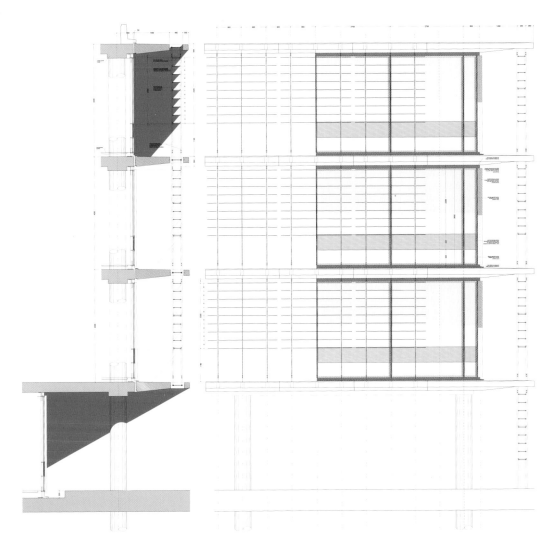

In CPA the number of louvres on each façade is determined by its orientation, as sun hits each façade at a different angle

→ see pages 172–177

extensive façade shading
In CPA's façade louvres, there are two films between two layers of glass. On the upper side, there is a reflection-diffusing white film and on the underside, a blue film. This sample was made to test and determine the colour of the under film

Architecture in Europe in 2010, among others. This was achieved through a mix of traditional, low-tech methods including fragmentation of overall massing into smaller linked volumes on a campus-type site, extensive façade shading, plus more sophisticated innovations including the *vigas frías*, or chilled-beam technology, which allows cold water to be circulated through the ceilings for cooling of median air temperature, with the aid of state-of-the-art chillers.

As Vidal says, this technology had never been implemented in a climate as hot as that of Seville, but the office was confident, on the basis of Arup's calculations, and in conjunction with other traditional methods of environmental design, that it would work. 'Innovation is always two or three steps ahead of technique,' Vidal has observed, and 'our technique is more about innovation and added value…' (LV 3.12). It is this position that has led the office to become engaged in the development of research projects for sustainable low-cost housing in South America, stressing the potential for use of recycled materials, and also for an original façade-design tool which would allow clients and architects to work through a rigorous analysis of any given environmental scenario, using a clearly

working together with Luis for 'The Sustainable Skin' was great. Façades that really work: isn't that worth investing in? IGNACIO FERNÁNDEZ

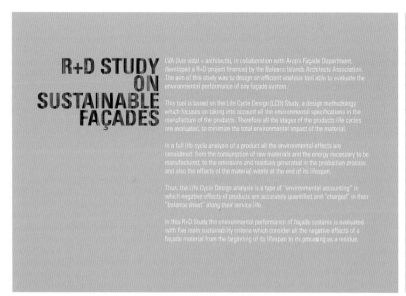

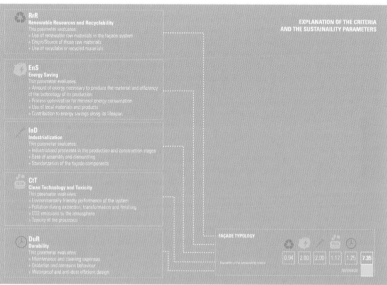

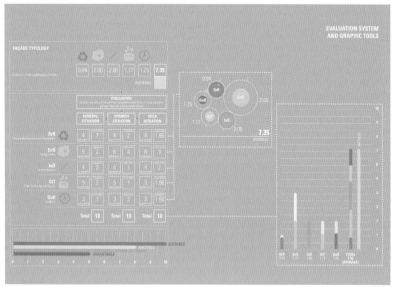

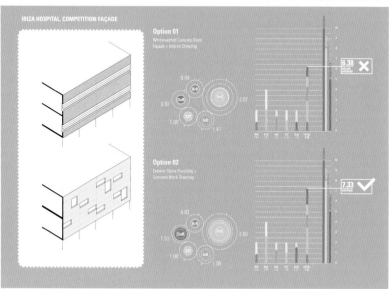

⬆ The Sustainable Skin

Excerpts from one of the reports on sustainable façades

➔ see pages 156–157

determined methodology, in order to diagnose an appropriate response.

This project, called The Sustainable Skin and developed together with Arup, was prompted by the office's response to the realization that many clients expected to be offered a ready-made proposal for the design of a building's façade, even before the various contributing factors had been established and analyzed as a basis for understanding how it might function at an optimum level. It challenges at the most fundamental level the idea that a building's external appearance, expressed in its façade design and specification, should be a matter of architectural aesthetics or branding, rather than a worked-through response to a particular set of circumstances and requirements. However, at the same time, it establishes the principle that well-designed, 'working' façades can act as a powerful advertisement for environmental responsibility, and an effective demonstration of the role of sustainable technologies and design in the production of building and place identity. The Abengoa pedestrian bridge, designed as part of the CPA, is a case in point: a delicately engineered, open-mesh metal tube structure incorporating a simple roof-covering, which shades the pedestrian route between the campus and the centre of Seville across a motorway, while creating a distinctive architectural intervention with a light touch, which gives an element of recognizability to the 'non-place' of the motorway environment.

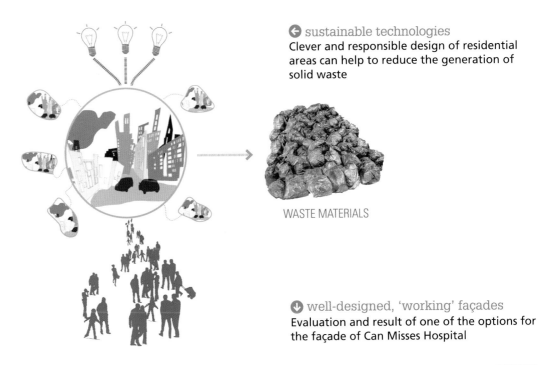

◀ sustainable technologies
Clever and responsible design of residential areas can help to reduce the generation of solid waste

WASTE MATERIALS

▼ well-designed, 'working' façades
Evaluation and result of one of the options for the façade of Can Misses Hospital

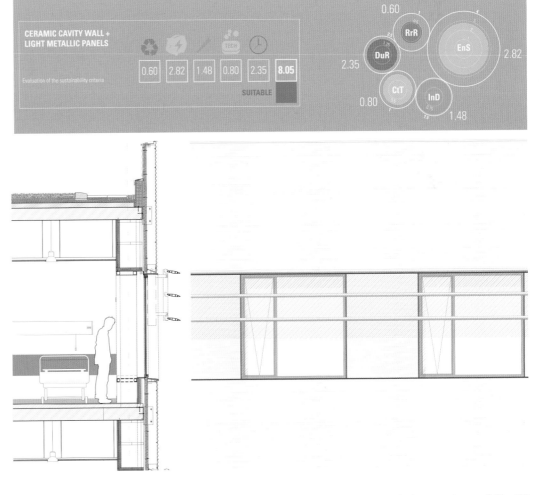

CERAMIC CAVITY WALL + LIGHT METALLIC PANELS

Evaluation of the sustainability criteria

0.60 | 2.82 | 1.48 | 0.80 | 2.35 | 8.05

SUITABLE

0.60 RrR
DuR 2.35
EnS 2.82
0.80 CtT InD 1.48

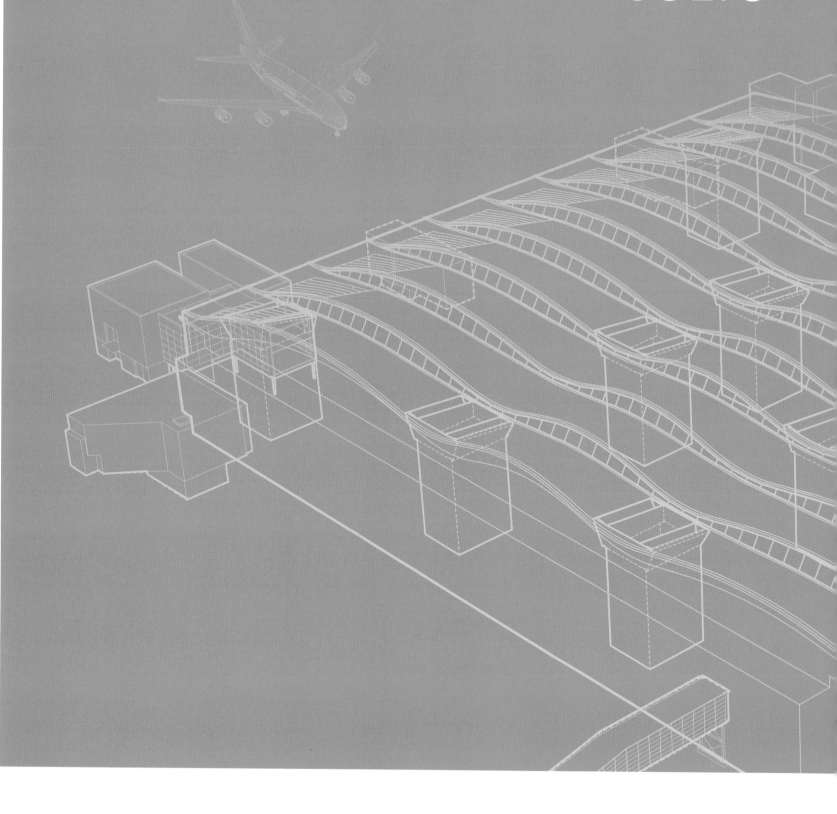

DESIGN LEADING TO RESULTS

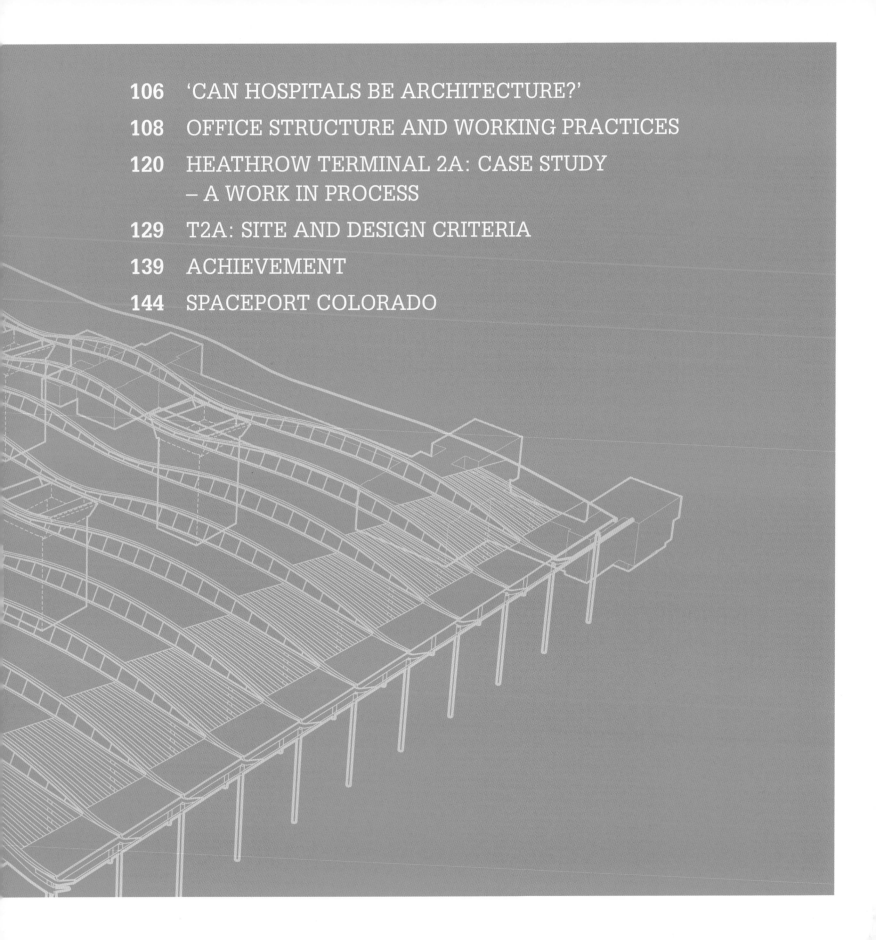

'CAN HOSPITALS BE ARCHITECTURE?'

This question reflects a common understanding that 'the functional and technical success of hospitals depends on the ease with which they can grow and change… The aesthetic implications of designing buildings whose ultimate extent and form cannot be predicted has received less attention' (James and Noakes 1994: 2). The 'long-life, loose-fit, low-energy' (ibid) approach has been perceived as a challenge to the relevance of architectural and aesthetic expression, while at the same time, the depressing standardization, institutionalization and bureaucratization of hospital design has attracted increasing criticism. 'Until the 1950s,' writes Cor Wagenaar, 'architects often succeeded in designing hospitals that were highlights of their urban and suburban surroundings, but after that they housed the medical world on an island isolated from the world outside' (Wagenaar 2006: 14).

These issues lie at the heart of LVA working practice across the range of contemporary, large-scale building types which largely implicate the same issues of standardization and bureaucratization identified by Wagenaar in the realm of healthcare. But the emphasis on approaching design practice as a process leading to results, as opposed to the production of preconceived architectural forms in line with a particular aesthetic position, underpins a commitment to working with clients – from doctors and hospital managers to airport directors – in order to explore the functional and technical problems of a brief collaboratively, and evolve corresponding forms of architectural expression which reintegrate those specialized and bureaucratic realms of society with 'the world outside'.

⊙ hospital design
Can Misses Hospital. The central spine connects with the existing building (to the left). Each pavilion houses a different speciality
⊙ see pages 182–187

⊙ process leading to results
The long route is hard but leads to a better building

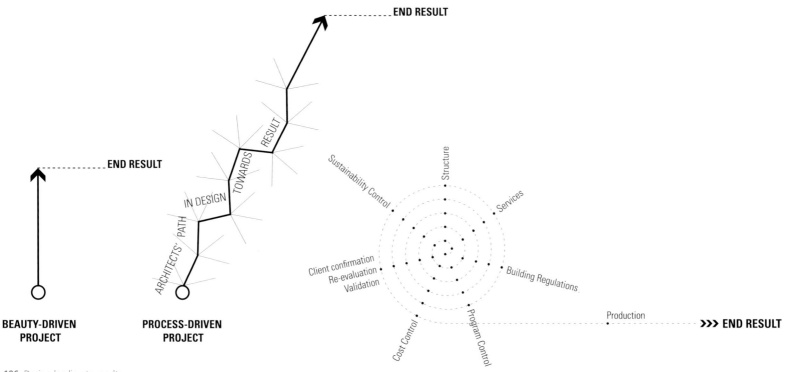

BEAUTY-DRIVEN PROJECT

PROCESS-DRIVEN PROJECT

END RESULT

ARCHITECTS' PATH   IN DESIGN   TOWARDS   RESULT

END RESULT

Sustainability Control   Structure   Services   Building Regulations   Program Control   Production   END RESULT   Client confirmation   Re-evaluation   Validation   Cost Control

you can only become aware of curative architecture when you are able to understand the needs of users and fulfil the requirements of clients MAGDALENA GARCÍA DE DURANGO

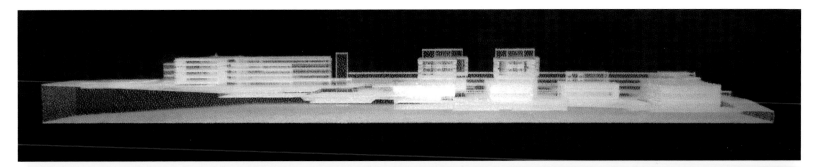

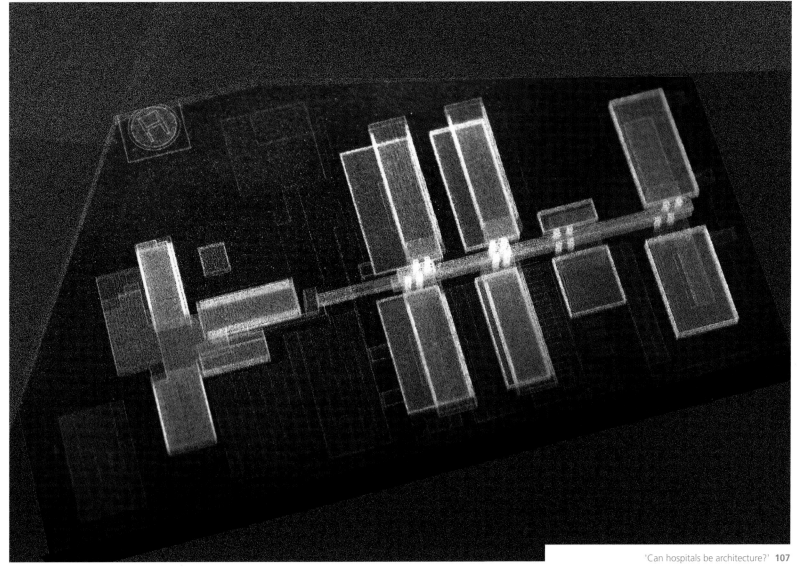

Luis was an encouraging tutor who did not push us into a design but allowed us to dream freely. He believed in our vision before even we did

#POLYTECHNIC UNIVERSITY OF MADRID — ANA SERRANO

OFFICE STRUCTURE AND WORKING PRACTICES

Vidal returned to Spain following the completion of his training in the UK in 1993. Employed to work on a winning competition design for a headquarters building for AENA, the Spanish airport authority, Vidal brought AutoCAD with him to the office in Madrid and set about revolutionizing working practices and repositioning the firm on an international platform. He also set up a regular weekly discussion event and an in-house magazine as a forum for the exchange of ideas, while teaching part-time himself at the Polytechnic University of Madrid. Following the decision to launch his own office in 2004, in shared premises with RSHP, Vidal has built on those ambitions and ideas to create a collaborative

⬇ Polytechnic University of Madrid
ETSAM School trip to Portugal in 2001. Siza, Souto de Moura, Porto, Lisbon...

⬇ his own office
LVA / RSHP new office main space at Velázquez 76–78 when the scaffolding-made tables arrived

working environment in which the client is framed always as an ally, and the approach to design development as an analytical and interactive procedure which generates a number of options, while also maintaining the intuitive spirit of the Mediterranean studio approach.

⬅ his own office

The meeting room can be cleared by hanging the tables on the wall. Both tables and chairs are LVA designs

a committed client, on time and on budget = Zaragoza Airport terminal: one of my best experiences ÓSCAR TORREJÓN

⬆ Óscar Torrejón
Oscar has worked with Luis Vidal for 13 years

⬆ different circumstances
Luis Vidal with Renzo Piano on a preliminary site visit to Santander

➔ see pages 194–197

Partner Óscar Torrejón has underlined the contrasts in expectation which architects encounter in working with an international range of clients and situations: 'a Polish client is happy if you just show you like being there, working with them. But you will have to convince a Spanish client; and prove to a British one' (OT 11.12). And, as Rogers and Smithson comment, you need 'a thick skin… to survive battles with contractors' in the UK (RR/SS 3.12). Therefore, Vidal's ability to understand and mediate situations, his 'good people skills', and commitment to maintaining personal contacts, are indispensable to the running of a successful office. In his own words, 'In order to be a useful person in this world, you have to have the ability to adapt to different circumstances' (LV 3.12). For many staff members, then, the experience of working at LVA is very different from the previous experience they may have had working in small Spanish studio practices, often employing no more than

⬇ international range
LVA has working alliances in Canada, USA, Colombia, Chile, Japan, Panama, Mexico, Peru, Italy and the UK

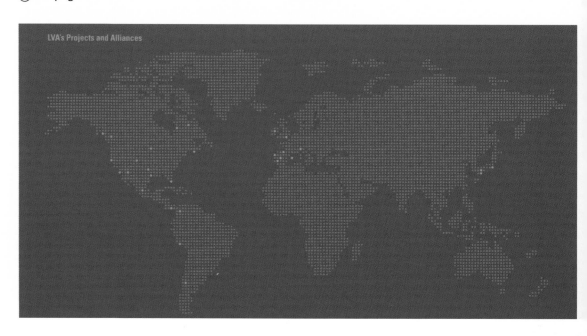

LVA's Projects and Alliances

← fully worked-out scheme
The site team for Seville's CPA project ensured that nothing was left to chance during construction
→ see pages 172–177

10 staff, many of them students, where the emphasis remains primarily on design and architectural expression and production of an architectural concept, rather than the multi-dimensional and technical process of working with clients (70% of whom are contractors) and specialist consultants towards a fully worked-out scheme for construction. Speaking of the Can Misses Hospital project, for example, where the office has conducted a large number of interviews with medical staff as part of its remit, one of the architects comments that 'doctors always ask for more' (3.12); and when managers are replaced, as they have been four times in this case, 'everything changes' (LV 3.12). Clients, and especially doctors – reflecting the specialization and bureaucracy of the medical world – can be demanding and opinionated about design. The architect's role, then, is to develop a good understanding of the way that their client's world works (for example, to know about an airport's three key areas of revenue: car parks, retail and aeronautical fees), and to find a way of translating the tension which can be generated into a fruitful and successful architectural proposition. For another of the architects, LVA embodies a 'business-oriented vision', which keeps 'things on the move' (4.12) in the office.

Modern architectural practice, then, is not just a case of sketching compelling ideas on napkins, but rather a complex and sometimes tortuous process of talking, proposing and working through ideas in teams, using efficient computer software and the latest technologies that can be proven to work. It means shifting in scale constantly between the over-arching picture – the site strategy within the context of an urban landscape, the technical infrastructure of a complex building, and its environmental and economic performance – to the minutiae of physical details which will have an enormous impact on the daily experience of future building users, for 'the magic is in the detail' (LV 3.12).

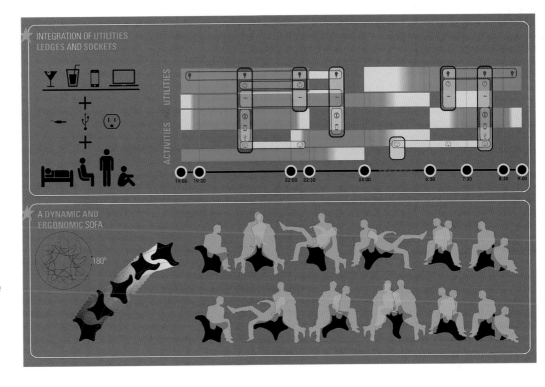

↩ proposing
Spaceport Colorado conceptual image by HDR and LVA

⬆ the detail
Twist is a modular sofa system that allows for working, relaxing and sleeping positions. It will be available in different finishes for domestic, office or commercial use

↩ ⬆ physical details
MOOD sanitaryware has recently been launched. Luis Vidal at the Bologna fair, checking out the final product

→ see pages 208–209

The LVA office structure is based on integrated teams working on particular projects, rather than individual staff working on specialized elements, which is, Vidal believes, a recipe for 'buildings working like machines' (LV 3.12). There is one Partner and four Associates at the time of writing, who simultaneously lead projects and assume different responsibilities for different fields of the office's operation – including design review; office co-ordination; new business, PR and publications; finance; IT; Quality Assurance certification; Green Group (environmental); and ongoing training.

Vidal's Partner Óscar Torrejón has responsibility for all the London operations, as well as for the contractual and legal side of the office's workload in association with Vidal. The Partners and Associates go on retreat together twice a year for two days, with invited junior architects, and this provides a valuable opportunity to review and shape realistic strategies for the office's future development in the short, medium and long term. It underlines the value placed on open debate and discussion within the office organization, which also forms a significant feature of the weekly work schedule, launched every Monday with a design review meeting at which different attendees are chosen from all levels by the team leaders to present their thoughts and opinions on the work in hand, in a collaborative and mutually supportive environment.

 Associates
Associate Jugatx López's strengths are in the co-ordination area

 London operations
Óscar Torrejón took these photos of Heathrow Airport from the air in January 2013. We can see how advanced the works for T2A and the T2B pier are (highlighted)

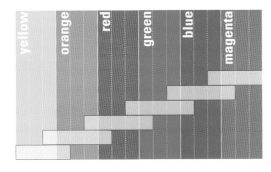

⬆ colour-coded system
In LVA the salary depends on the category but it is flexible: reward depends on professional value

⬇ individual voices
Office organization meeting

Staff members' different roles in the office are categorized by a colour-coded system, which includes magenta, blue, green, red, orange and yellow-coded architects, depending on their level of responsibility and seniority in the team, magenta being the colour equivalent to an Associate. However, their freedom to choose colours and the design for the back of their own round-shaped business cards is indicative of the office's loose and flexible approach to hierarchical organization, which provides scope for individual voices to be heard, as well as for staff to move around within the structure of the office and seize the opportunities that suit them as they arise.

As several members of the office 'family' concur, this offers a very special situation which is rarely found in architectural offices, especially at a larger scale. There is always the danger for younger architects of being relegated into a specific role which circumscribes future development, and often resentment at the sense of being exploited as 'CAD monkeys'. At LVA, by contrast, there is always the opportunity to learn about architecture and working processes, even in the context of bigger projects, supported by internal processes of knowledge exchange and shared expertise. LVA consistently funds ongoing training for its employees, for example in the use

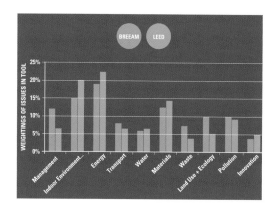

⬆ BREEAM and LEED
This is a comparative study of BREEAM and LEED criteria for certification

⬇ different people
The LVA / RSHP Madrid team in Valladolid, March 2013

of Revit and also in BREEAM and LEED standards for environmental design, for which LVA provides specialist in-house consultation services – its Green Group also represents an integral component of its internal Quality Assurance process. It also maintains up-to-date information on the latest products, systems and technologies, which is communicated to the whole office in order to ensure that everyone is in the best position to make appropriate proposals and choices when it comes to design decisions and specifications. Furthermore, the office offers an experience of the very substantial technical and regulatory side of architecture (particularly significant in the UK, and especially by contrast

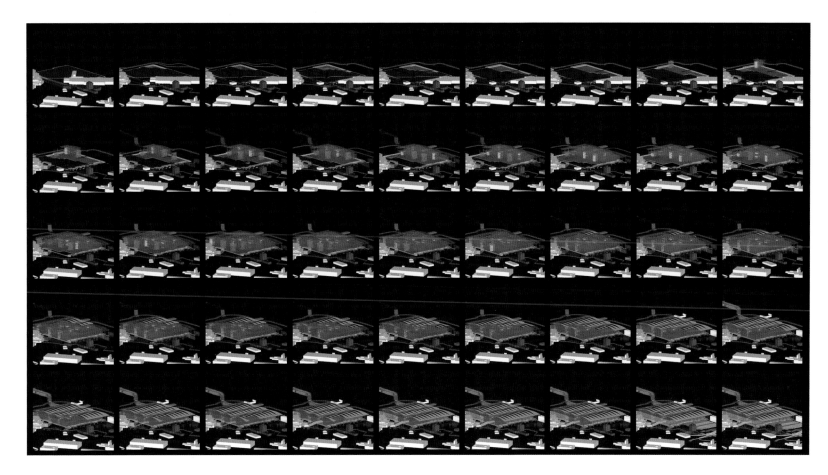

with Spain), which is recognized by existing and prospective staff and sought after as a distinct advantage over their peers, especially in the Spanish context. 'We're very young for the type of things we're doing… working in a system with many different people, dealing with huge amounts of information and very strict bureaucratic systems… how to draw the project, deliver it, quality control…,' explains one of the blue-coded architects (11.4.12) of the Heathrow T2A project. The experience engenders a strong sense of responsibility, and an understanding of tight and well-structured construction programmes. 'It makes you focus on what you really want – you can't overproduce, you have to focus. It purifies the design process… things are built as we design them,' adds an orange-coded architect: 'At university you're educated to explore a lot, but you have to stop it at a certain point.' Making presentations to 30 people in the Design Leadership at BAA, dealing with maintenance specifications, CDM, fire regulations, adds up to 'a big learning experience', which is possible because Vidal and Torrejón 'have trusted us… it's a great opportunity'. Ultimately, 'being able to take important decisions and manage a team is more important' than being part of a big 'starchitect' practice; 'the important thing is the project you're working on, rather than the office.'

The climate of freedom and opportunity within the office is reflected in the relative lack of any tailored or fixed 'house style' governing either the use of particular architectural references, or the production of drawings and visual material by the practice, or

⬆ construction programmes
Building sequence for the T2A building

⬇ Vidal and Torrejón
Luis and Óscar during the construction of the Zaragoza Airport terminal
↪ see pages 168–171

indeed the specification of particular materials or fittings. Cited precedents may be historical, geographical or cultural, as much as architectural; someone may present material from a trip to share with the rest of the team, and the international make-up of the office contributes to a broad scope of reference. When it comes to drawing style, the practice at LVA contrasts with that of RSHP, which has very clear policies about presentation and checks all output on collaborative projects for readability and house style. Staff at LVA are free to work in their own style, sketching by hand and making physical models, before translating material

into electronic form. There's no office style as such, but at the same time it is a 'perfectionist' approach, which underlines professional quality, the need for proposals to be put together logically as well as be 'pleasing to the eye' and, above all, to be 'interesting for the city, the neighbourhood, wherever it fits…' (LV 12.11). Likewise, there is no restriction on the catalogue of elements, the palette of materials and finishes that may be used. The emphasis is on using whatever suits the project and works most efficiently, at the right cost, rather than a concern for aesthetics or a particular shape or look.

⬆ ➡ no office style
A small sample of the office's variety of presentation styles. Opposite clockwise from top left, Spaceport Colorado conceptual plan by HDR and LVA; façade for housing in Vallecas; a pylon situated in the landscape; and RS chair concept sketches. Above, the geometry behind the Vallecas façade

the beauty of LVA's work is an extension of the way they work – lively, unencumbered, passionate, connected. You're anxious to be included STEVE RIOJAS

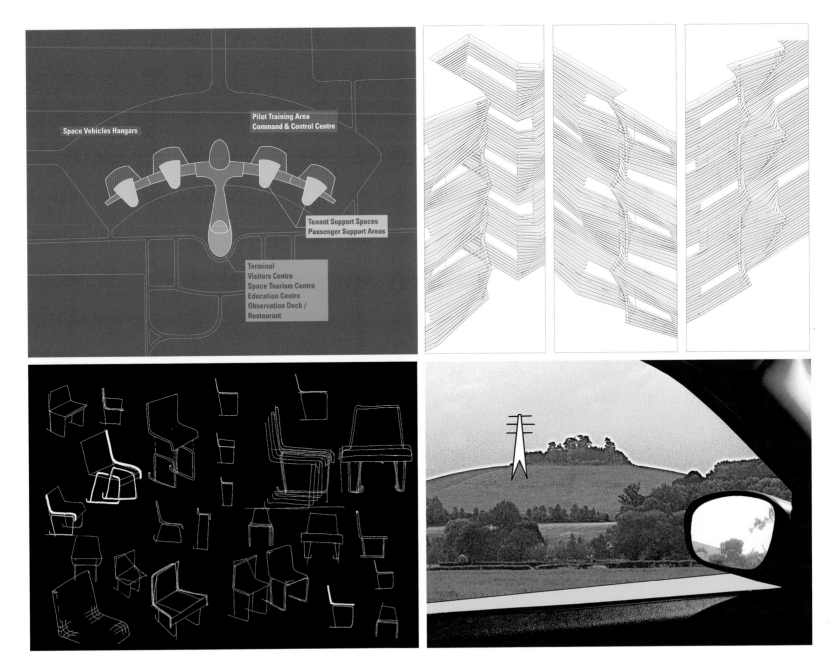

HEATHROW TERMINAL 2A: CASE STUDY – A WORK IN PROCESS

The project for Heathrow T2A very much embodies the aspects of the office's working processes described in this book. In the words of Fran Rojo (one of the Associates at LVA), the development of the scheme from 2008 for contractor HETCo (a joint venture between Ferrovial and Laing O'Rourke) was 'a great challenge for our team, in which the interaction of parties, both internal and external, constituted one of the main pillars of its success' (10.12).

It was preceded by an earlier proposal, Sprint 11 – which constituted the basis and concept for the later Sprint 33, now T2A – produced at the request of BAA as an alternative proposition to a scheme by Foster + Partners. F+P's 2007 scheme, responding to the schedule of facilities and areas set out in BAA's brief, was considered too expensive and complicated, a building that could not meet the fixed cost and construction programme.

In less than a week, Luis Vidal put a team to work at full speed, supervised by Óscar Torrejón, who had successfully led the design and construction of the Zaragoza Airport terminal and several other airport terminal design competitions, all of which had tight schedules and budgets. The T2A LVA team expanded to a total of 20 people in late December 2007. Made up not only of architects but also engineers, the team worked when and where it was best for the project, in this case BAA's offices in London. Sprint 11 was a more economical scheme which featured

→ Sprint 11
Floorplans of the Sprint 11 option for the Heathrow T2A building
→ see pages 160–167

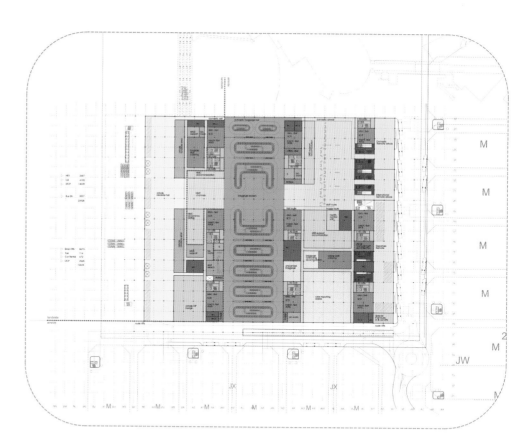

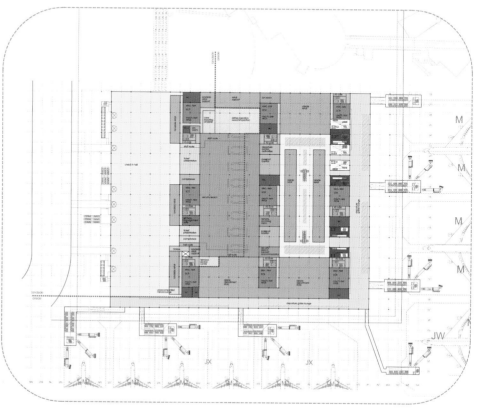

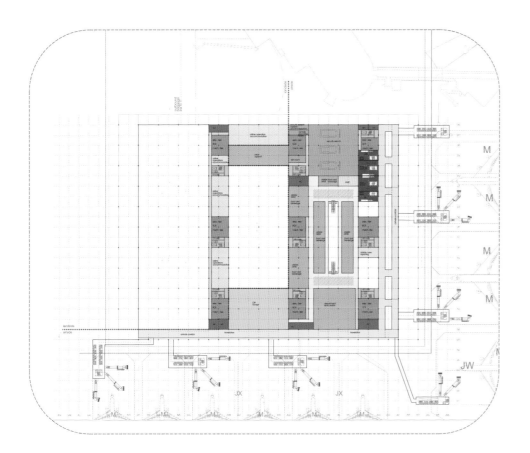

↑ Óscar Torrejón
OT at the Zaragoza Airport terminal site during construction

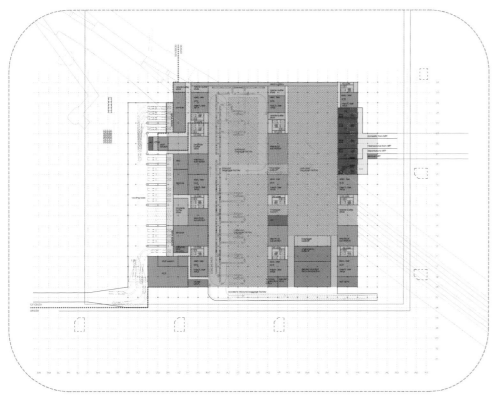

the direction of Heathrow T2A has taken 100% of my last five years. The result is very good, but still better the memories recorded within ÓSCAR TORREJÓN

a dramatic undulating roof wrapping round glazed illuminated boxes. Like the Foster proposal, it provided for a naturally well-lit internal space, but formally it embraced a more fluid, organic and less geometric approach to the envelope. In addition, it considerably reduced the height and size of the module, overlapping some of the internal areas, to economize on the volume of the building.

BAA gave LVA just seven weeks to work up the project: they worked to the limit in order to deliver a project that could be costed and evaluated in terms of construction programme. But above all, they kept in mind BAA's recurrent brief: a design to produce a terminal which would be recognized not only as an airport, but also as a gateway to London.

The project was presented to BAA's Directors in December 2007 and an independent consultant confirmed that it met the cost target and the construction programme. The design was highly

⊙ dramatic undulating roof
The roof was conceived as 10 ribbons wrapping the building

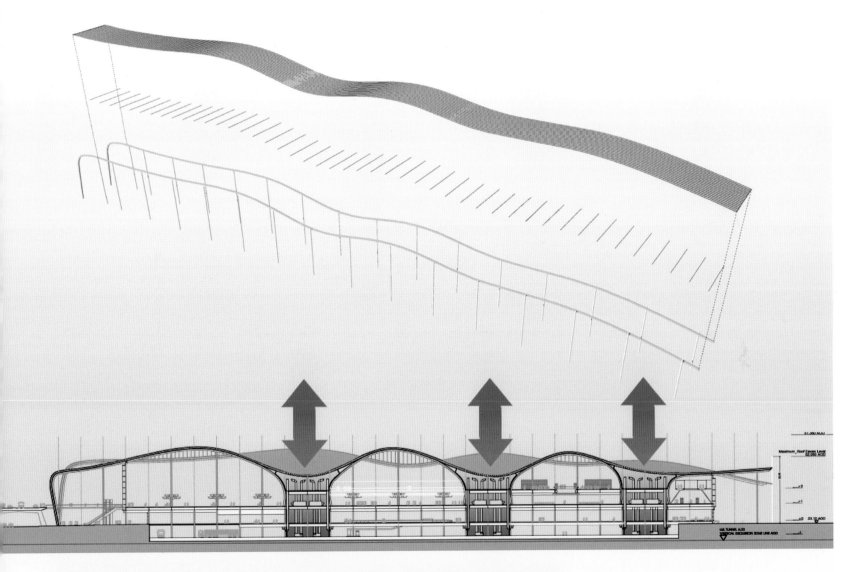

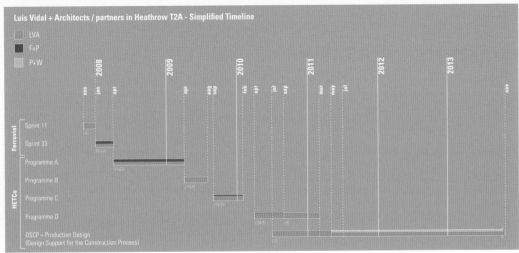

Luis Vidal + Architects / partners in Heathrow T2A - Simplified Timeline

↑ glazed illuminated boxes
The glazed boxes served also as service courtyards, simplifying enormously the task of bringing fresh air into the building

← seven weeks
Timeline of the work of LVA on the Heathrow T2A building

acclaimed by most of the members of the board. However, Vidal was aware that this situation was sensitive, and therefore suggested setting up a joint venture with Foster + Partners to develop LVA's concept together; this was named Sprint 33 ('sprint' being the term used by BAA to describe design exercises run in parallel to the main work; there were no other sprint exercises between Sprint 11 and Sprint 33).

This joint venture agreement was based on three principles: unanimity, mutual respect and an equal division of effort, resources and fee between the two architectural practices.

It took less than three months to achieve a sign-off from BAA and HETCo for the adaptation of Sprint 33 from Sprint 11.

⬆ joint venture
For the Programme A phase, LVA, F+P and HETCo shared premises in Madrid. The team comprised up to 100 people

⬇ Long section of the Sprint 33 design. The three 'waves' guide the users through check-in to security control, and then to the departures lounge

➡ Sprint 33
Floorplans of the Sprint 33 option for the Heathrow T2A building

↪ see pages 160–167

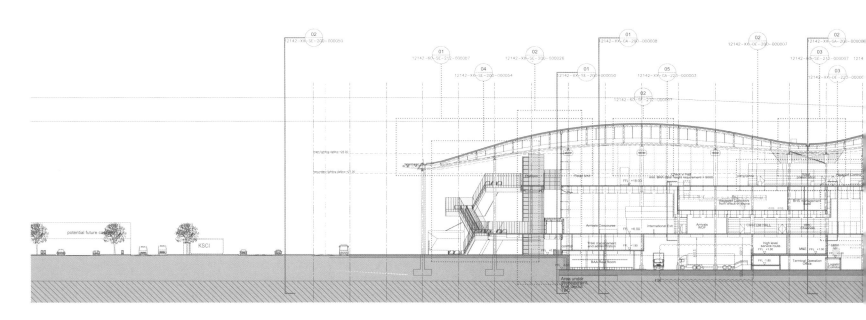

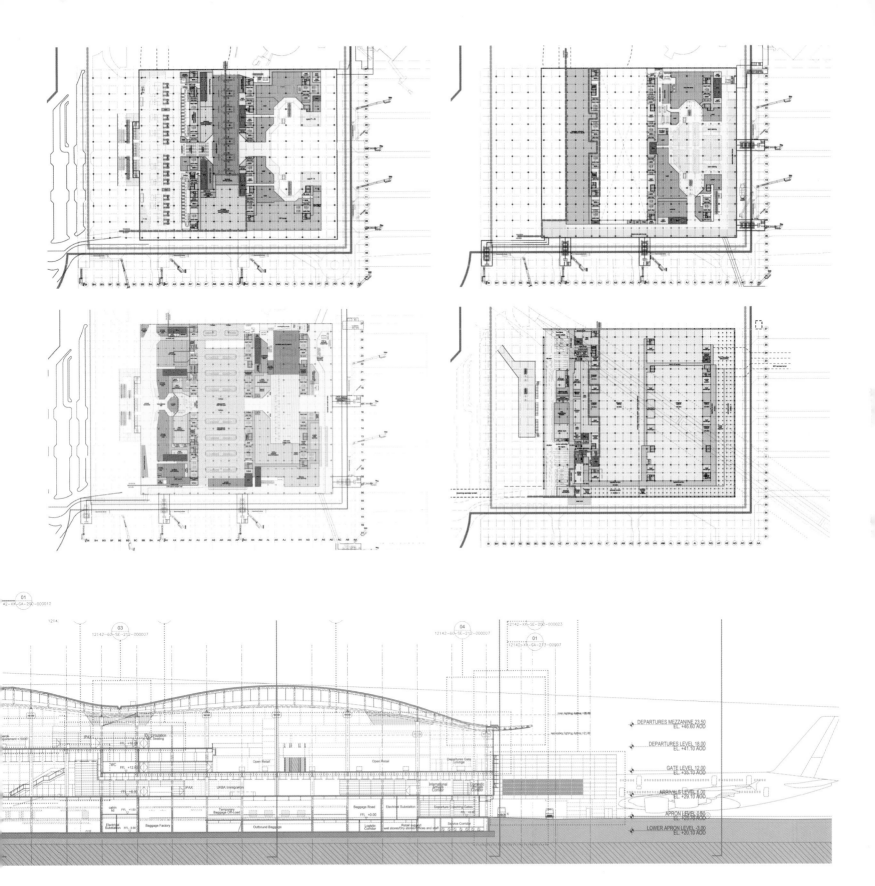

⊕ **Programme B**
Programme B represented a study at a finer level of detail, involving the development of the interior fit-out space planning and design. It was established to engage with the Development Managers and Stakeholders at a one-to-one level

⬇ **more than 15 options**
Every option was costed and checked for construction feasibility

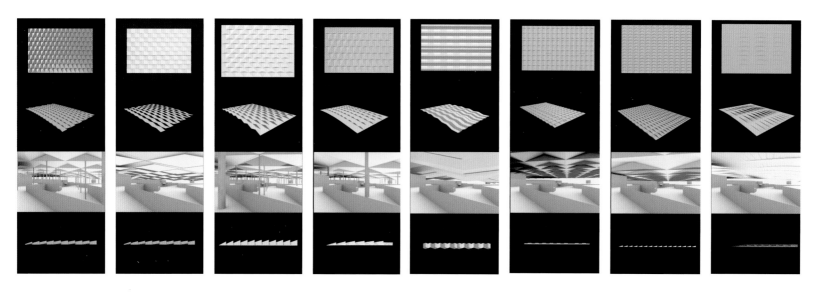

⬅ ➡ **office on site**
The Heathrow T2A site supervision team in London consisted of more than 20 people at the beginning of the works

#OFFICE ON SITE the best thing on such a big project is the team. We learn from everybody; it´s enriching

MARÍA ÁLVAREZ-SANTULLANO

More than 15 options for the conversion of the roof were explored before work started on schematic design and design development stages in April 2008 (Programme A, running through to February 2009), with the whole team now located in Madrid at that point. In April 2009, however, BAA asked the team to modify the scheme, and LVA worked alone on Programme B until August, before F+P rejoined the project in September 2009 to develop a further modification, Programme C, until February 2010. Between April 2010 and March 2011, LVA worked alone again on Programme D of the project, and on DSCP (Design Support for the Construction Process) from July 2010 onwards, relocating the team to London once again in July. Fifty architects were installed in an office on site at Heathrow shared with consultants and client representatives, in order to supervise construction and liaise more effectively with their client, HETCo, and with the architects for the Main Terminal fit-out, Pascall + Watson.

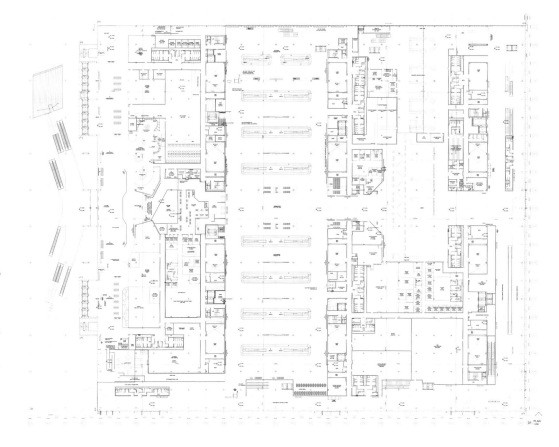

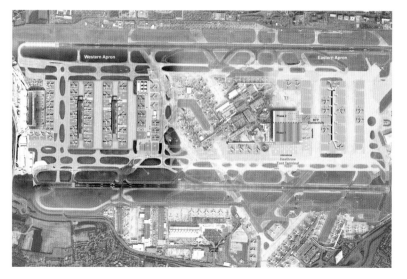

⬆ highly constrained
LHR Airport showing T2A on the right-hand side. Future expansion includes extension of T2A and its connection to the T2B pier, which is under construction at the time of writing

⬆ Site boundaries as defined in the Outline Planning Application

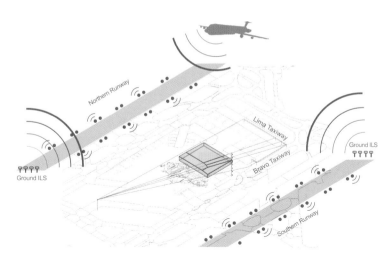

⬆ T2A could not interfere with the Instrument Landing System. For this reason, the south façade had to be inclined by exactly 15 degrees

⬇ The sightlines from the Control Tower had to be respected and the building could not block the 23cm radar waves. The building had to be lower on one side than on the other

⬆ Below-ground constraints included the Piccadilly Line tunnel

Visual Control Tower

Visual Control Room Sight Line

23cm Radar Limit   62.00 AOD

Central Terminal Area Buildings   38.30m   East Terminal Site   29.50m

Piccadilly Line Exclusion Zone

Piccadilly Line Tunnel

T2A: SITE AND DESIGN CRITERIA

The new terminal is built on the site of the former Terminal 2, Flight Connections Centre and Queens Building, as part of an initiative to replace the old facilities to the east of the Central Terminal Area, which started with the opening of Terminal 5 in 2008. It will replace its neighbour, Terminal 1, which will eventually be demolished. The site for the new building was highly constrained and one of the requirements of the brief was that it should be fully integrated with existing public transport links, particularly with the underground rail system. In addition, care had to be

taken not to interrupt the 23cm radar limit associated with the Instrument Landing System and the existing Visual Control Room sightlines. This meant that the height of the building would have to be lower on the east façade than the west.

The principal concerns were to accommodate the site constraints effectively, and provide the best passenger experience possible, notably through the provision of more natural light and space inside the building than normal, and operating conditions which would allow for an enhanced level of customer service. Check-in

⊙ more natural light and space
View from the mezzanine onto the commercial area. We begin to see the space taking shape

was designed to be easy, the departure lounge relaxed, and boarding procedures open and integrated: 'Passenger experience remains in people's memories. Heathrow's T2 will become one of the main gateways (both leaving and entering) of the UK. And that is precisely why we have worked very hard to mark the difference, to leave that impression when travelling through Heathrow's Terminal 2. Passengers react in different ways and moods, affected by different factors: time, company, business, leisure, connecting flights… But there are also common factors that affect people: the quality of light, acoustics, textures and colours perceived, comfort, ambience, legibility of the building (understanding what comes next) or way-finding, as well as views to the exterior where they can orient themselves and understand the weather outside …' (Luis Vidal 12.12). In addition, the flexibility and modularity of the design had to allow changing future demands on the space to be accommodated. All of these were concerns that had been explored extensively and addressed by LVA in its earlier airport design projects, in conjunction with a strong emphasis on the need to achieve an environmentally

↑ Luis Vidal
Luis during the first visit to the site for Seville's Campus Palmas Altas

#DEC 2010 LHR is closed due to a snowstorm. The LVA family plans to spend Christmas in London together HÉCTOR ORDEN

↓ distinctive undulating design
Evolution of the London Heathrow T2A design over time, from initial stages to construction. From left to right: LVA's concept 2007, LVA's concept development with F+P, LVA's construction output

The building works started with the structure from the south-east corner module in the summer of 2010. Photo taken December 2010

responsible building through the implementation of active and passive systems and renewable energies – including recycling 80% of the concrete from the previous building on the site.

The LVA / F+P scheme developed from Sprint 11 adopted a more linear character, also based on a modular approach to allow for the scheduled Phase 2 extension of the envelope in 2020 replacing Terminal 1, and also for ease of assembly during the construction process. The structural module size was reduced from the original 24m to 18m, to produce a more economical volume. But it is the tangible sense of flow through the building from west to east which makes it different from models such as Stansted, and which is given strong visual expression in the distinctive undulating design of the roof structure, evocative of Zaragoza.

'The roof is the prominent feature of Terminal 2. Conceived as a lightweight

⬆ three sections
This north-facing façade will be dismantled and recycled when the extension to T2A is built

⬅ 'shark's-gill' openings
Image of a shark next to a 3D recreation of the T2A roof

structure resembling the early aeroplanes, a floating series of wings pivoted towards the north provide climate protection while allowing natural light penetration. This feature is unique and contributes significantly to the reduction of solar gain inside the terminal, thus reducing energy consumption' (LV 12.12). The three sections, or 'waves', of the roof define the progression of the passenger-processing flow through the spaces within, from west to east – from arrival under the roof canopy overhanging the forecourt, to check-in, through security, and then to IDL (International Departures Lounge). The roof structure is built on an 18m x 18m bay, within which the covering is designed as a series of successive, north–south orientated sections, allowing for top-lighting of the departures floor via north-facing glazed clerestories, or 'shark's-gill' openings, which provides enhanced natural illumination to the interior. Originally these were designed to face west, running in parallel with the 'wave' form of the roof, but in order to reduce solar gain they were rotated 90 degrees to face north, creating a counterpoint of ripples to the main direction of flow, and helping to reduce energy consumption in the building by 40% compared to current legislation in the UK (part L Building).

The underside of the roof is covered by a translucent and reflective soft-fabric soffit containing silicone, almost like an artist's canvas, which diffuses natural and artificial light, reducing excessive brightness, and enhancing the perception of the lightness and spaciousness of the main public concourses. The sophisticated design ensures that glare-free daylight illuminates the space all the way from check-in to aircraft boarding, and that the terminal does not overheat in the sun, while an LED system inside it simulates natural

↑ translucent and reflective soft-fabric soffit
A sample module of the soffit put in place as mock-up and being supervised by LVA prior to its approval

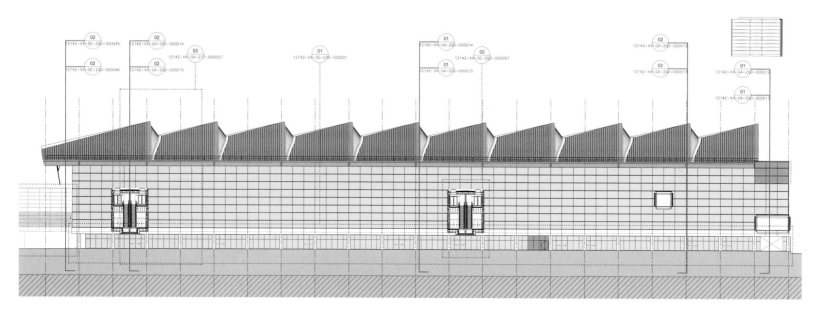

🔽 glazed façade
South façade, during construction

🔼 Section through the FLANs (Fixed Links and Nodes) and south elevation

➡️ angled louvres
Mock up of the façade and louvres. Each louvre measures 1m x 3m and weighs 100kg

as Native Americans weave their dream-catchers, Luis Vidal captures not only the clients' needs, but also their dreams PATRICIA ROJAS

light to supplement the effect on grey London days.

The glazed façade of the envelope was also designed to enhance the internal brightness and transparency of the terminal, but incorporates solar-control glass and angled louvres, with an overhanging roof shading the south-facing windows. The disappointment for the architects was the need to design a transfer tube for domestic arrivals passengers passing in front of the façade on the south side, following the changes requested by BAA in Programme B — notably the relocation of domestic arrivals from the east to the south façade. The tube effectively obscures the line of vision out of the terminal through the façade from within; but on the other hand it creates a plane of transparencies which has its own interest.

#FAÇADE **for us it is a great pleasure to work with Vidal. His designs are balanced on functionality and efficiency, and they stand the test of time** ELADIO CUIÑA

The module for the glazing components was derived from that used at Zaragoza, which was identified as being the optimum for the fabrication of the glass (3m x 2m panels), avoiding the need for a massive vertical structure to support the façade. By contrast, the structure is equipped with cables embedded in the joints, designed not to produce an overt aesthetic effect, but simply for functionality. Although BAA initially had doubts about the design, preferring the concept of a vertical façade, LVA were able to demonstrate that the concept was not complicated or expensive, but an example of efficient, pragmatic design, which would ultimately cost less.

As an example of value engineering, the louvres that shade the façades reduce solar gain but also serve to conceal the joins between the plane FLANs and the terminal wall. The additional shading in the south façade

⬆ module
General view of the east façade with its overhang to protect from morning sun

⬅ efficient
The design had to allow for glass panel replacements to be made after construction

is achieved by a system of aluminium rods that eliminates the need for a lot of supporting structure, due to its light weight. In addition, 600 square metres of photovoltaic panels on the canopy, shading the covered courtyard, provide a source of renewable energy, which contributes to the terminal's energy-saving profile.

All the mechanical and engineering (M&E) and service systems were prefabricated, while the metal structure was assembled on site. The scheme was designed and developed by an integrated working group, based at the contractor/client's offices in Madrid. As Partner Torrejón points out, the fact that architects, engineers, consultants and client representatives from HETCo were all based in the same space was hugely advantageous in terms of eliminating delays in communication, and facilitating

○ aluminium rods

An aluminium-rod grille is suspended from the roof and creates shading

○ M&E and service systems were prefabricated

The 12 cores were built off-site in 15 segments each. They contain air-treatment units and other mechanical and electrical systems

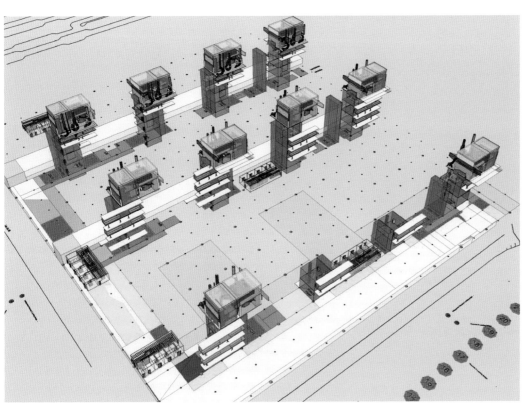

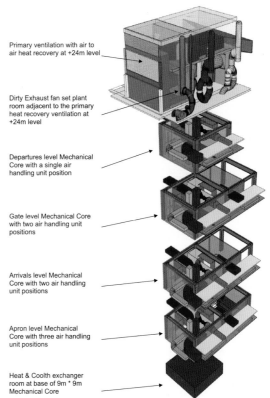

Primary ventilation with air to air heat recovery at +24m level

Dirty Exhaust fan set plant room adjacent to the primary heat recovery ventilation at +24m level

Departures level Mechanical Core with a single air handling unit position

Gate level Mechanical Core with two air handling unit positions

Arrivals level Mechanical Core with two air handling unit positions

Apron level Mechanical Core with three air handling unit positions

Heat & Coolth exchanger room at base of 9m * 9m Mechanical Core

when an architect sees his ideas taking shape, meridian sun strikes the upper surface of his soul MARTA CUMELLAS

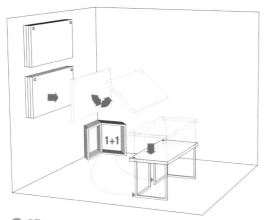

↑ 3D
Foldable tables and easily movable partitions designed by LVA

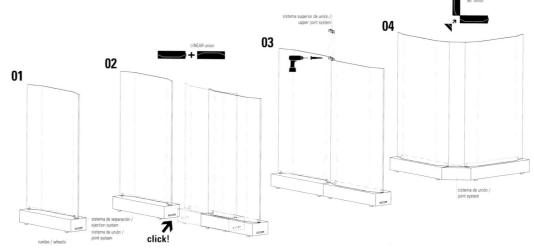

01

02

LINEAR union

03

04

90° union

sistema superior de unión /
upper joint system

sistema de unión /
joint system

sistema de separación /
ejection system
sistema de unión /
joint system

ruedas / wheels

click!

BAA Heathrow East Terminal
Budget Challenge Team Alternative
November 2007

↑ Cover of the Budget Challenge Team Alternative – also known as Sprint 11 – presentation

↑ need to draw
Marta Cumellas sketching alternatives based on Zaragoza Airport terminal

collaboration on the development of the construction system, components and assemblage. Also, for the first time in LVA's history, the scheme was designed and developed in 3D from the outset, using Revit and BIM, following the lead of the suppliers. As Torrejón observes, 'it is the future', in terms of construction co-ordination, although at the same time he stresses, 'We are architects, we still need to draw'; indeed, there was a sense that, because of the compressed time-frame of the project, the team started to work exclusively on the computer too early on, notwithstanding the sustained use of working physical models in cardboard, and finished, realistic models in wood and plastic for presentation to the client, which characterizes LVA practice.

ACHIEVEMENT

With the capacity to process 20 million (rising to 30 million once Phase 2 is completed) passengers per year, Heathrow T2A will be a building on a grand scale which must work to maximum efficiency in every aspect of its functionality. But, in common with all LVA's projects, the total assemblage of its components is intended to surpass a merely mechanistic analysis of its functionality and environmental credentials, and offer passengers, staff and visitors an experience of pleasure

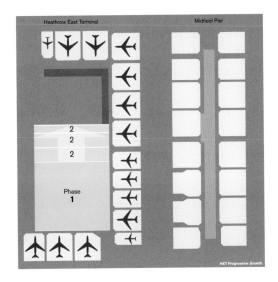

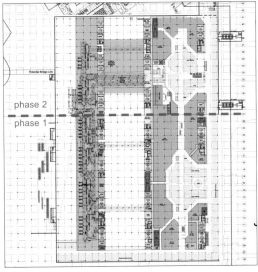

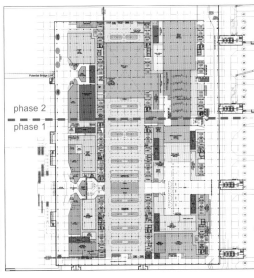

 Phase 2

From day one the plans for future extension of the building have been taken into account. This will minimize the cost and disruption and will result in a cohesive final image

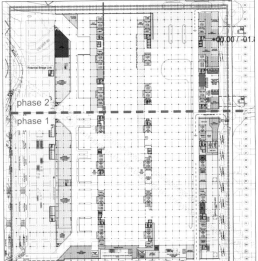

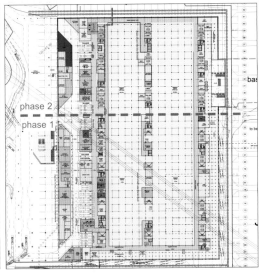

↑ not just architects

The LVA T2A on-site team is a very close-knit group of professionals who show their creativity in many ways

↓ the team

LVA's team on the Terminal 2A site

↑ Francisco Sanjuán

Paco Sanjuán travels non-stop, supervising the construction works of Can Misses and Vigo Hospitals

and well-being in its environs, as a very important hub for international air travel. It is an outlook which views and embraces the many participants in an architectural project as equally important actors in the story of its realization – not just architects themselves. As LVA Associate Francisco Sanjuán observes, 'what satisfies me the most in this profession is to see the material of our work finished… not on paper, but to see how it is understood by thousands of participants: architects, engineers, economists, doctors, administrators, politicians, foremen, carpenters, etc.' (FS 10.12).

In the case of LHR T2A, LVA came under considerable pressure to show that they could produce a cost-effective scheme which could nevertheless equal the quality and architectural panache of a project by a much larger, very high-profile office. The team pulled together to draw on the full extent of its potential and show moreover that it could engage successfully with the British construction and project management system. As Sanjuán puts it, 'the result was spectacular [and]… our satisfaction with the objectives we achieved is immense… we are not only satisfied with the result, but also inspired by the challenge we faced, which was to overcome the present economic situation and become a top international office' (FS 10.12).

⬇ the result was spectacular
The terminal is 200m by 190m long, and 27m high above ground level

◑ ◐ Fran Rojo

Fran Rojo shuttles between Madrid and Santander to supervise the construction of the Botín Centre

⊙ see pages 194–197

◐ Isabel Gil

Associate Isabel Gil was the first architect to join LVA in 2004. A former pupil of Vidal at university, she has spent most of her career at LVA on healthcare projects

D
E fficiency
s
i
g
SPAIN
n
n
o
v
a
Technology
T
i
o
n

⬆ EDIT=E
Very preliminary conceptual sketches for the exhibition

Sanjuán explicitly describes the working method as 'empirical and scientific, in which the greatest number of options possible was analyzed and subjected to a process of internal dialogue', and 'the construction company, through its subcontractors, actively participated in the development of the project.' However, it was a challenge to work in this way, demanding a willingness to explore new territory – in the words of Fran Rojo (Associate), 'large doses of youth, boldness and freshness' were required, but in many ways it is these qualities which are key to the profile of the office and differentiate it from others. After all, 'Architecture is like cooking; the best dishes come from challenging the recipe, while the best buildings come from challenging the brief,' states Vidal, and only by pursuing such a bold and questioning approach can architects hope to transform space into place through the medium of architectural design.

It is little surprise, then, that as this book goes to press, Luis Vidal has been given the go-ahead to curate an exhibition titled EDIT=E (Efficiency, Design, Innovation and Technology = España). The exhibition will take place in Japan between

October 2013 and July 2014, as part of Spain's Year in Japan. Funded by the Spanish government and private companies, the exhibition will explore the theme of technological innovation and responsibility, in parallel with a commission from Sumitomo to design an innovative urban transportation system linking four towers 500m apart in a new development in Tokyo's harbour area.

'In the end,' observes Associate Isabel Gil, 'the studio is a grand project, constantly evolving, that does not just adapt to changes but provokes them, being a creator of innovation. All of the projects are distinct, and as such, are treated uniquely; we tailor each opportunity where everyone is called to participate: the client with their needs, the consultants with their wisdom, and of course, the team with their magnificent experience… Every day we learn from each other, from the clients, consultants, colleagues and friends, to improve the ways we do things, the way we confront the challenges we face and how we resolve them… we make the process as open and proactive as possible, making each of the solutions much more enriching and interesting and always giving an added value to the final product' (IG 10.12).

↪ best buildings
London Heathrow T2A south façade before
the construction of the FLANs

↓ we tailor
The west-facing canopy provides shelter at
the entrance to the terminal building

SPACEPORT COLORADO

The spaceport is the logical next step in the evolution of transport infrastructure, embracing both high-speed suborbital flights and the extension of earth's connections to other parts of the universe for travel, tourism and cargo transport. The US currently has eight spaceports in action, and LVA's most recent project is a competition-winning scheme for a new facility in Colorado, in partnership with engineering firm HDR. Colorado Governor John Hickenlooper compared the outlook for the development of spaceport infrastructure to the opportunities represented by mobile phones in the 1990s, which seemed far-fetched at the time, but radically transformed personal communications within less than a decade. In terms of space-travel technology, the development of dual-propulsion (jet- and rocket-powered) spacecraft, or 'space-planes', capable of taking off horizontally from a conventional runway, has completely altered the outlook for the development of the aerospace industry. In the US, commercial spaceports are regarded as a natural complement to an already highly developed air-transport system, opening up the potential to travel between continents within a couple of hours, as well as farther afield into space.

The LVA/HDR design solution proposes to incorporate not only a terminal, but also a Visitor Centre, Education Centre, Space Tourism Centre and Observation Deck/Restaurant, underlining the public-education dimension of such a facility. There is also a pilot-training centre and flight simulator. Designed for phased construction in four stages, with the potential for further expansion in the future, it could provide up to five space-vehicle hangars capable of accommodating multiple space-vehicle types.

as we cruise towards the next century we must respond to the planet's challenges with social, economic and environmental responsibility LUIS VIDAL

→ new facility in Colorado
LVA / HDR conceptual image of
Spaceport Colorado

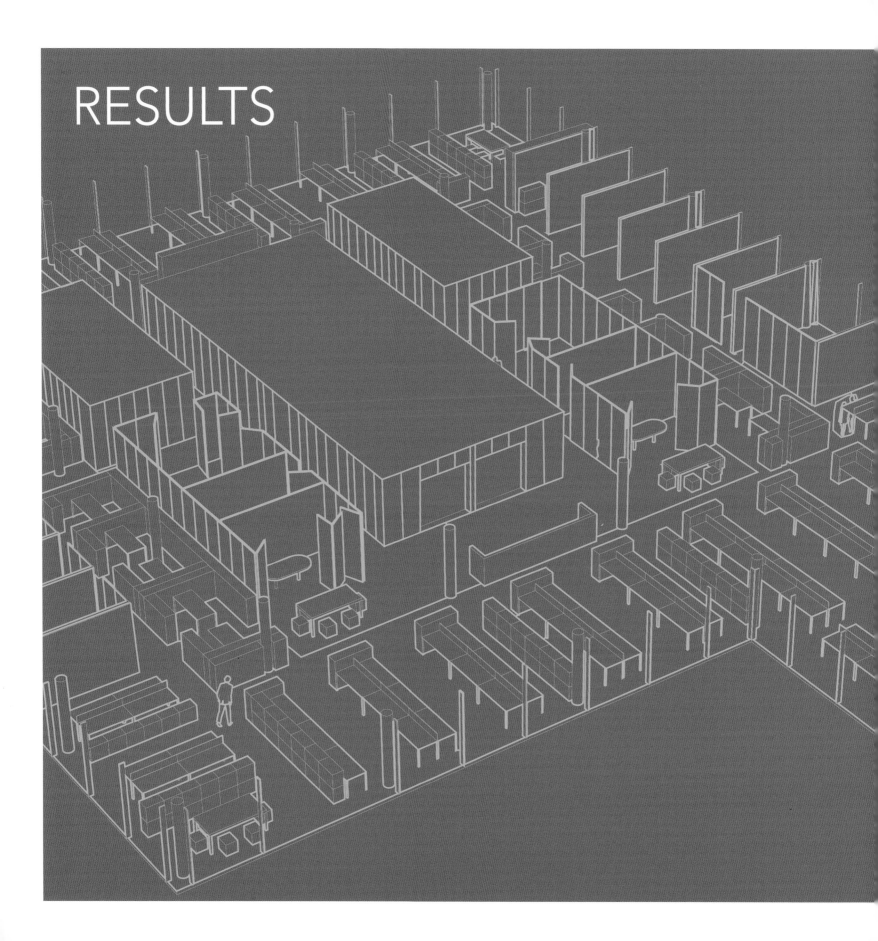

RESULTS

URBAN DESIGN VALLADOLID MASTERPLAN (WITH RSHP)

1 The central area is organized around remarkable industrial buildings from the 19th and early 20th century, related to the old railway

2 View of the new public spaces around the transport hub

3 View of the new boulevard

4 Inhabitants of these areas will be five or ten minutes walk from the new linear park

5 The new green spine will connect the city centre with its surrounding large-scale parks

1

Place	Valladolid
Date	2005–2020
Client	ADIF and Ayuntamiento de Valladolid (Valladolid City Council)
Architects	Luis Vidal + Architects / Rogers Stirk Harbour + Partners
Area	980,000sqm
Stage	Final approval of the General Plan Amendment
Awards	First prize in international open competition by Valladolid Alta Velocidad. First prize in Urban Regeneration and Masterplanning Award in MIPIM Future Projects Awards 2009

2

3

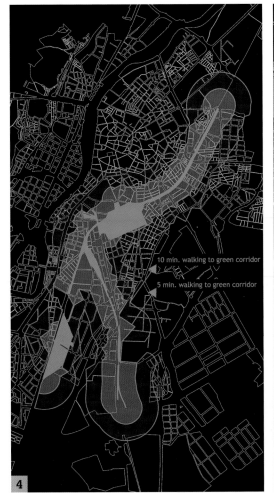

10 min. walking to green corridor

5 min. walking to green corridor

4

5

Valladolid is the capital of the Castilla–León region of Spain, 200km north-west of Madrid. With 400,000 inhabitants, it has been divided in two by a railway and adjoining rail industry land for over 100 years. Due to very poor road connections between the two sides of the city, the social and economic levels on each side are radically different.

With the decision taken by central government to run the railway underground and to move freight rail and associated industry out of the city centre, new opportunities arise. Two big pieces of land (one of them very central) will be sold for development in order to pay for the infrastructure works. A public open competition was proposed to choose a team to manage the development.

The project objective was to reconnect the city and regenerate the most marginal and least favoured parts of it with new intensive landscape and mixed-use land distribution.

A single and continuous boulevard, more than 4km long and up to 60m wide, mixing elements which will enrich the social and cultural life of the city, is to be created. The boulevard will contain a pedestrian route through green spaces and small parks, a bicycle lane, and areas for new small public buildings, intended for local use. Also, it will feature a segregated bus lane, which reinforces a new strategy for public transport in Valladolid and its surrounding settlements. The fast bus lane will go through a new bus station, which will also be connected to the train station for easy interchange.

Three new neighbourhoods will be created in former rail-industry areas. All three will combine housing, public facilities, parks and public spaces, and commercial use, in different proportions depending on the needs of each area. The most interesting industrial buildings will be retained and adapted for new uses while keeping the memory of those work spaces.

This is a sustainable project twice over, first in environmental terms and second in economic terms.

6

7

8

6   View of the public space in front of the station and shopping mall

7   Train station and bus hub

8   View of the Argales area

9   City view corridors

10 Urban mobility system strategy

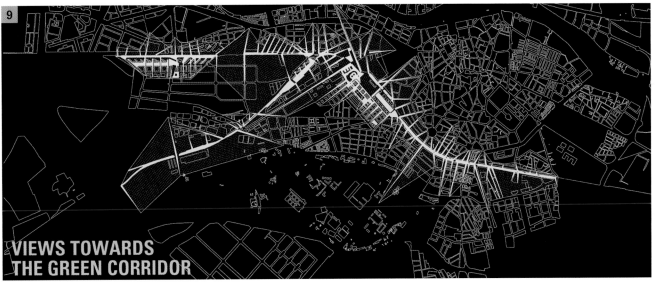

9

VIEWS TOWARDS
THE GREEN CORRIDOR

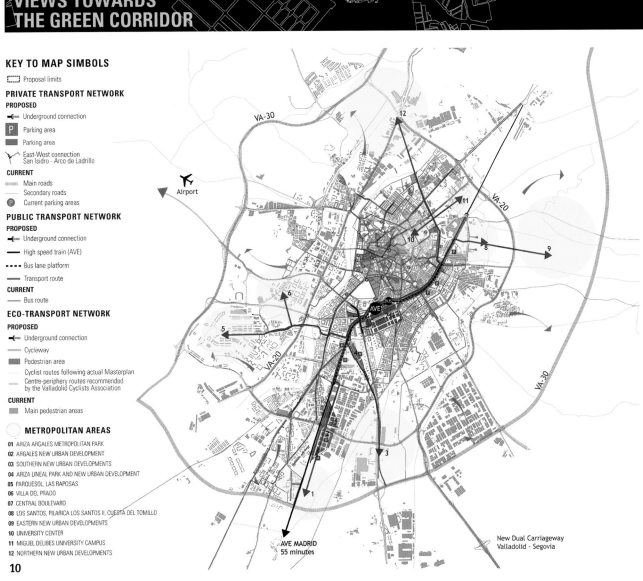

KEY TO MAP SIMBOLS

⌐⌐⌐ Proposal limits

PRIVATE TRANSPORT NETWORK

PROPOSED

◄▦▬ Underground connection

Ⓟ Parking area

▬ Parking area

⋎ East-West connection
San Isidro - Arco de Ladrillo

CURRENT

▦▦▦ Main roads

— Secondary roads

Ⓟ Current parking areas

PUBLIC TRANSPORT NETWORK

PROPOSED

◄▦▬ Underground connection

▬▬ High speed train (AVE)

•••• Bus lane platform

▬▬ Transport route

CURRENT

— Bus route

ECO-TRANSPORT NETWORK

PROPOSED

◄▦▬ Underground connection

▬▬ Cycleway

▦▦▦ Pedestrian area

— Cyclist routes following actual Masterplan

— Centre-periphery routes recommended
by the Valladolid Cyclists Association

CURRENT

▬ Main pedestrian areas

◯ METROPOLITAN AREAS

01 ARIZA ARGALES METROPOLITAN PARK
02 ARGALES NEW URBAN DEVELOPMENT
03 SOUTHERN NEW URBAN DEVELOPMENTS
04 ARIZA LINEAL PARK AND NEW URBAN DEVELOPMENT
05 PARQUESOL, LAS RAPOSAS
06 VILLA DEL PRADO
07 CENTRAL BOULEVARD
08 LOS SANTOS, PILARICA LOS SANTOS II, CUESTA DEL TOMILLO
09 EASTERN NEW URBAN DEVELOPMENTS
10 UNIVERSITY CENTER
11 MIGUEL DELIBES UNIVERSITY CAMPUS
12 NORTHERN NEW URBAN DEVELOPMENTS

10

LA MARINA MASTERPLAN, SAN SEBASTIÁN DE LOS REYES (WITH RSHP)

1 Comparative size study of famous parks around the world, in order to get the scale right

2 Permeable edges concept

3 Nighttime during the fair

4 Daytime, normal use

5 Aerial view; the size of the new park is clearly seen

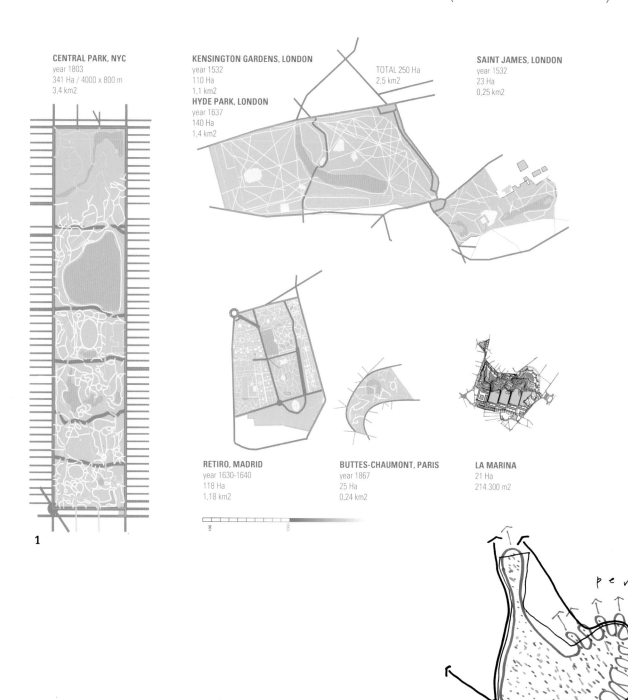

CENTRAL PARK, NYC
year 1803
341 Ha / 4000 x 800 m
3,4 km2

KENSINGTON GARDENS, LONDON
year 1532
110 Ha
1,1 km2

HYDE PARK, LONDON
year 1637
140 Ha
1,4 km2

TOTAL 250 Ha
2,5 km2

SAINT JAMES, LONDON
year 1532
23 Ha
0,25 km2

RETIRO, MADRID
year 1630-1640
118 Ha
1,18 km2

BUTTES-CHAUMONT, PARIS
year 1867
25 Ha
0,24 km2

LA MARINA
21 Ha
214.300 m2

1

2

Place	San Sebastián de los Reyes (Madrid)
Date	2009
Client	San Sebastián de los Reyes City Council
Architects	Luis Vidal + Architects / Rogers Stirk Harbour + Partners / Ezquiaga Arquitectura, Sociedad y Territorio
Area	370,000sqm
Stage	Partially completed
Awards	First prize in international open competition by San Sebastián de los Reyes City Council

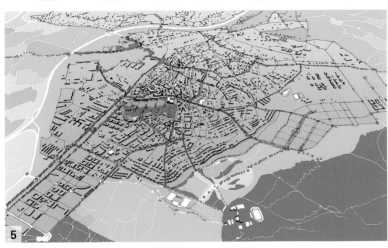

Originally an independent urban entity, San Sebastián de los Reyes is now one in a series of satellite cities north of Madrid.

The Ministry of Defence (more accurately the Spanish Navy, thus the name of La Marina) owned a disused and very big piece of land in an extraordinarily central location near the bullring in San Sebastián de los Reyes. The city brokered a deal with the navy in order to be able to regain the land. The terms included that the navy would receive a percentage of the profits that any future business established on the site might generate.

The brief was open and called for a sustainable proposal that incorporated economic equilibrium, meaning that revenue for the council needed to balance running costs.

The masterplan is based on the creation of a landscaped park in order to gather and consolidate the city in a much wider context. This green lung is incorporated into a network of green spaces, bike lanes and pedestrian corridors that go from Madrid to Alcobendas (a neighbouring town) to San Sebastián de los Reyes and on to the Sierra de Guadarrama, the chain of mountains north of Madrid. The plan also includes a number of building sites on the perimeter of the site to house mixed-use developments.

Looking at increase of building density, the proposal is rooted in achieving a complex and functionally diverse centre, with the capability to attract citizens to this area in particular, and to San Sebastián in general, making La Marina a destination.

A low-maintenance series of terraced areas will accommodate temporary structures during the festival dates (San Sebastián de los Reyes has many open-air markets), municipal events and activities during holiday seasons.

The buildings are placed at the edges, reinforcing the existing built axes and street life with shopping and housing-related activity, and are well integrated with the existing strong public transport network. The plan places the new bullring at the core of San Sebastián de los Reyes, hosting a schedule full of municipal activities and events.

The project has been put on hold by the client while they look for private investors and funding.

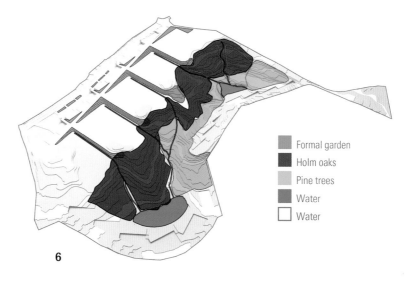

Formal garden
Holm oaks
Pine trees
Water
Water

6

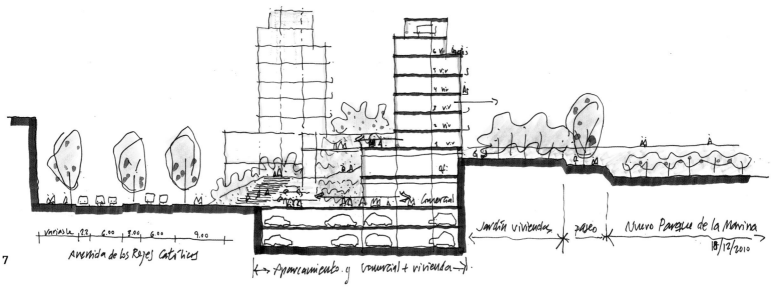

7

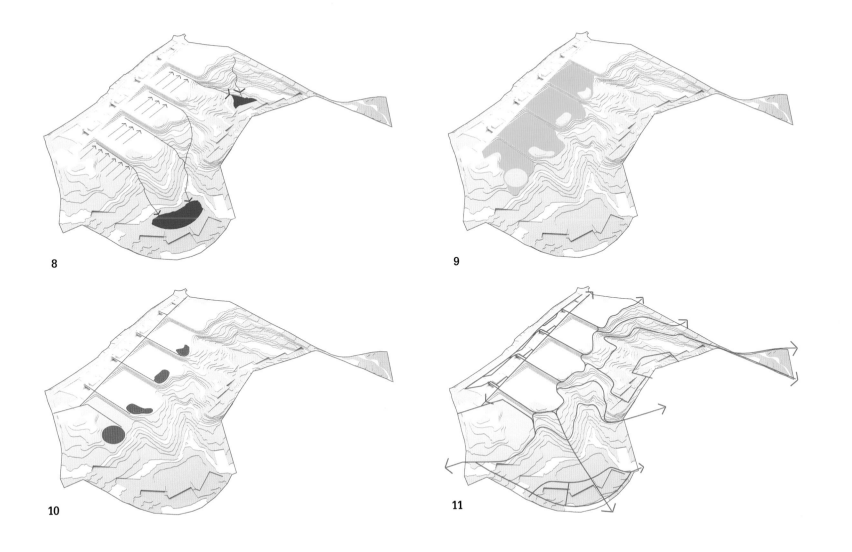

8

9

10

11

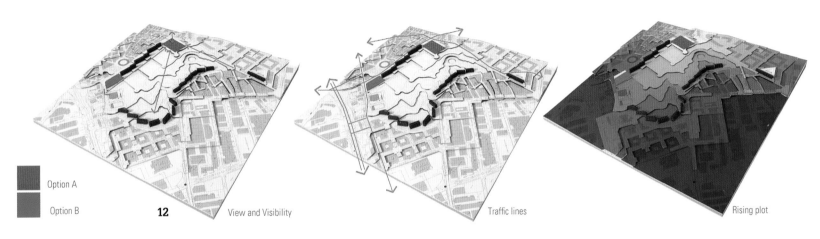

Option A

Option B

12   View and Visibility   Traffic lines   Rising plot

RESEARCH AND DEVELOPMENT
BUILDING ENVELOPES

1. Simple diagrams show the weight of all criteria taken into account, making comparison and evaluation very intuitive

2. Can Misses Hospital. The tool, used during project development, helped identify specific needs and thus design specific solutions

3. Vigo Hospital. The tool was used from the start to achieve a high-efficiency, low environmental footprint building envelope, which was part of the brief

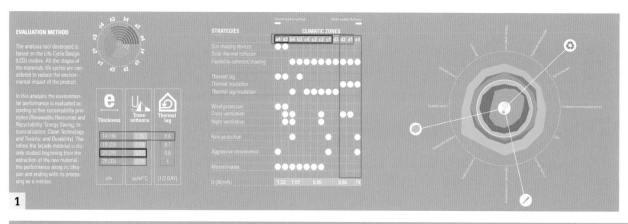

EVALUATION METHOD

The analysis tool developed is based on the Life Cycle Design (LCD) studies. All the stages of the materials life cycles are considered to reduce the environmental impact of the product.

In this analysis the environmental performance is evaluated according to five sustainability principles (Renewable Resources and Recyclability; Energy Saving, Industrialization; Clean Technology and Toxicity; and Durability). Therefore the façade material is closely studied beginning from the extraction of the raw material, the performance along its lifespan and ending with its processing as a residue.

1

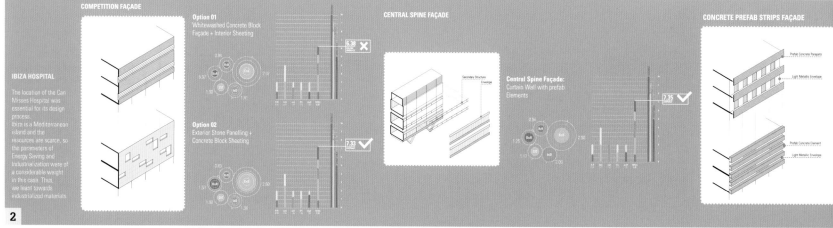

IBIZA HOSPITAL

The location of the Can Misses Hospital was essential for its design process. Ibiza is a Mediterranean island and the resources are scarce, so the parameters of Energy Saving and Industrialization were of a considerable weight in this case. Thus, we leant towards industrialized materials.

COMPETITION FAÇADE

Option 01
Whitewashed Concrete Block Façade + Interior Sheeting

Option 02
Exterior Stone Panelling + Concrete Block Sheeting

CENTRAL SPINE FAÇADE

Central Spine Façade:
Curtain Wall with prefab Elements

CONCRETE PREFAB STRIPS FAÇADE

2

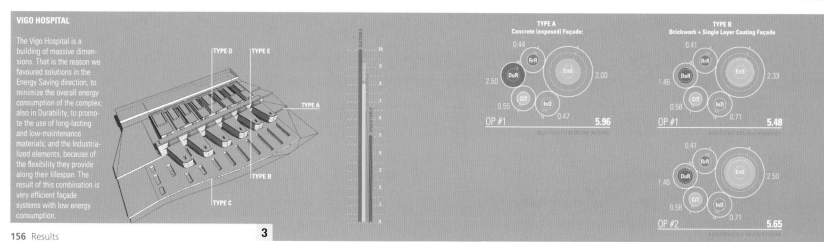

VIGO HOSPITAL

The Vigo Hospital is a building of massive dimensions. That is the reason we favoured solutions in the Energy Saving direction, to minimize the overall energy consumption of the complex; also in Durability, to promote the use of long-lasting and low-maintenance materials; and the Industrialized elements, because of the flexibility they provide along their lifespan. The result of this combination is very efficient façade systems with low energy consumption.

TYPE A
Concrete (exposed) Façade:

OP #1   5.96

TYPE B
Brickwork + Single Layer Coating Façade

OP #1   5.48

OP #2   5.65

3

Place	Madrid
Date	2005–2007
Architects	Luis Vidal + Architects
Stage	Research study completed
Awards	Awarded funds by the Balearic Islands Chamber of Architects. Finalist at 2009 Sacyr Awards (Environmental Innovation)

Building envelopes are not only a question of aesthetics. They have a big impact on the construction and running costs of a building. This project was born of the desire for a tool to inform façade design from the outset. The objective is to research and develop new sustainable and low-cost building envelopes.

Initially, the research was guided by three main themes:

Improvement of existing materials: both in their components and uses, studying the manufacturing process and end use.

Study of new materials: search for a new, sustainable material such as bamboo, canvas, textiles or duralmond (a composite using crushed almond shells).

Incorporation of active/passive systems into façades: considering the façade as a complex system that can be affected by a dynamic process, providing it with the capacity to respond to external factors.

Developed in close collaboration with Arup Façades, the tool can be used both for designing and testing. Evaluation assesses five aspects of sustainability:

- Use of renewable resources and recyclability
- Energy savings, in manufacturing the material or in a building's running costs
- Degree of industrialization of the system, to cut energy use and cost
- Ease of use and clean disposal at the end of the building's life
- Life-span and ease of maintenance, to reduce costs.

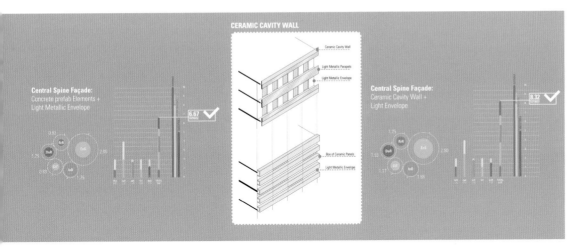

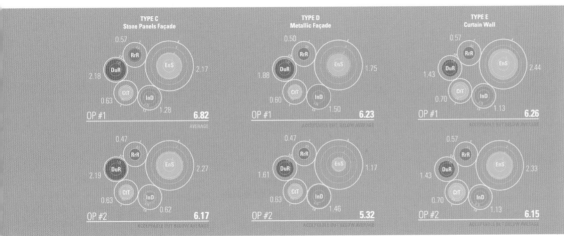

SOCIAL HOUSING IN SOUTH AMERICA

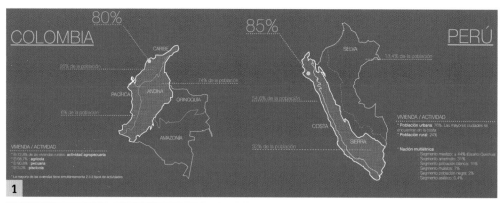

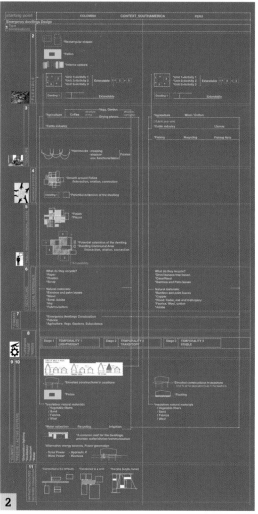

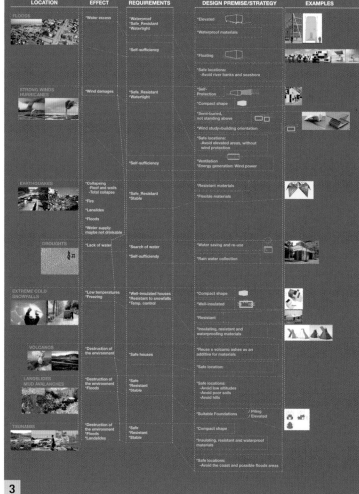

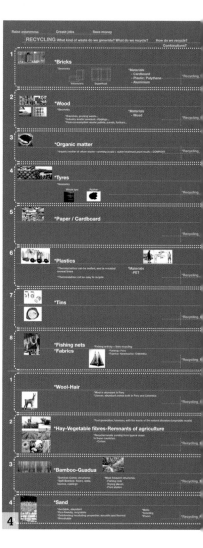

Place	Colombia and Peru
Date	2011
Architects	Luis Vidal + Architects
Stage	Research study completed

The objective of this research was to study prefab systems as a starting point for the definition and development of emergency housing. The focus was on sustainability in order to offer a better solution than any existing in the market. This type of housing is the paradigm of social responsibility for an architect.

Research was carried out considering the context and need for such housing, the requirements it needs to meet, and the necessary tools for its design. To be climate-specific, the framework was narrowed to South America, focusing on Colombia and Peru. The proximity of these countries to tectonic-plate junctions makes them prone to earthquakes, volcanic eruptions and landslides. They also suffer from floods and, in the case of Colombia, forest fires.

The research took into consideration the country context and the conditions that influence the design process, such as indigenous construction methods and the climate.

Emergency housing must be self-sufficient to ensure comfort for the inhabitants in extreme situations, often without power. The first step to achieve this is to minimize energy consumption with an architectural design adapted to the local weather conditions.

Also, research was carried out into light prefabricated components, flat-packing, the life cycle of materials and their recyclability, taking into account local construction methods.

This study provides a basis for the efficient development of prototypes and solutions for these countries.

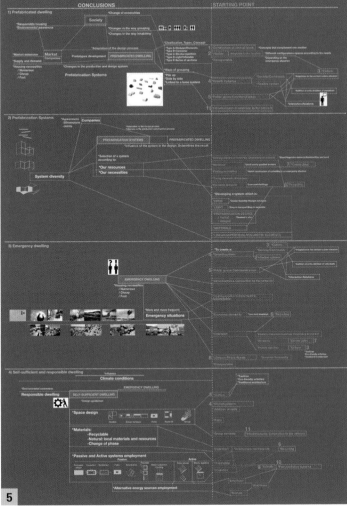

AIRPORTS HEATHROW AIRPORT TERMINAL 2A (WITH F+P)

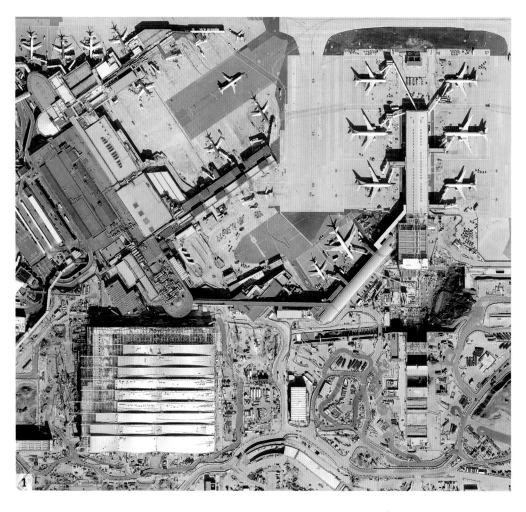

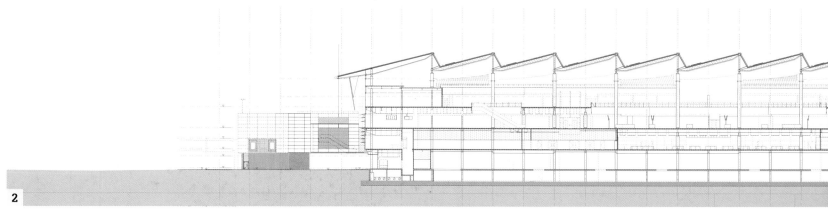

Place	London
Date	2008–2013
Client	HETCo (joint venture between Ferrovial and Laing O'Rourke)
Lead Architects	Luis Vidal + Architects (February 2008–November 2013)
Collaborations	Foster + Partners (Project phase: February 2008–January 2009 and September 2009–January 2010) and Pascall + Watson (fit-out: June 2011–November 2013)
Area	210,000sqm
Stage	On site

Built on the site of the former Queens Building and Terminal 2, the new T2A building (formerly called Heathrow East Terminal or HET) will be a first-class terminal capable of processing 20 million passengers per year. The budget is £880 million.

LVA first conducted a detailed analysis of the different pathways of people, aircrafts, materials and baggage in order to conceive a terminal that could manage millions of interacting flows in the most efficient, fast and reliable way, under the most strict security levels.

The new T2A is defined by a roof whose three large waves emphasize the three main parts of the process passengers go through before flying: check-in, security control and boarding. Therefore, function and form are deeply integrated, allowing passengers to orientate themselves easily through the terminal in an intuitive way. The roof waves lean against each other, housing skylights in their intersections. These skylights are directed towards the north to allow the entry of daylight, while reducing solar gain and thereby contributing to energy efficiency.

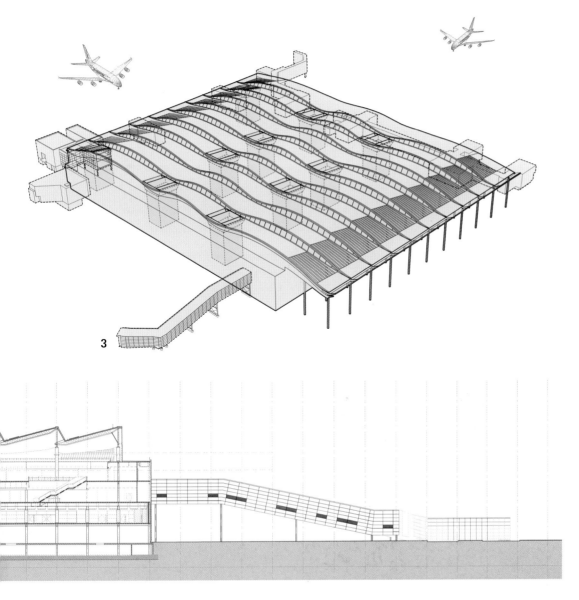

3

The proposed construction method minimized the impact on existing facilities and on the urban surroundings. This was possible thanks to innovative solutions based on modular systems and through a carefully considered construction schedule.

The departing passengers will enjoy more than 20,000sqm of retail space distributed over two floors, adjoining the boarding gates and offering excellent views to the embarkation platform.

The design reduces CO_2 emissions by 40% compared to a similar type of building, through the application of a combination of active and passive energy systems.

Flexibility and ease of expansion were starting points for the client and are guaranteed by the final design. After almost three years of intensive architectural design, at the time of writing LVA continues to provide design and co-ordination services to the main contractor and subcontractors.

There is more information about this project on pages 120–143.

4 Access to the terminal

5 South façade

6 Detail of south façade

7 View of the commercial area under construction

8 3D illustration of façade systems

4

5

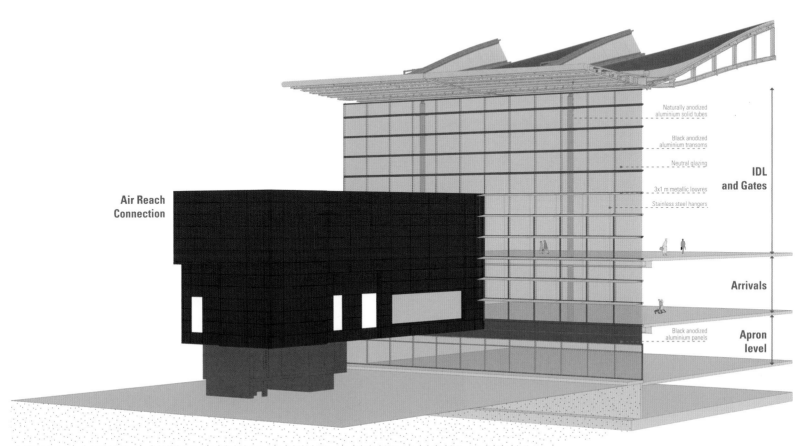

Air Reach
Connection

Naturally anodized
aluminium solid tubes

Black anodized
aluminium transoms

Neutral glazing

3x1 m metallic louvres

Stainless steel hangers

Black anodized
aluminium panels

**IDL
and Gates**

Arrivals

**Apron
level**

8

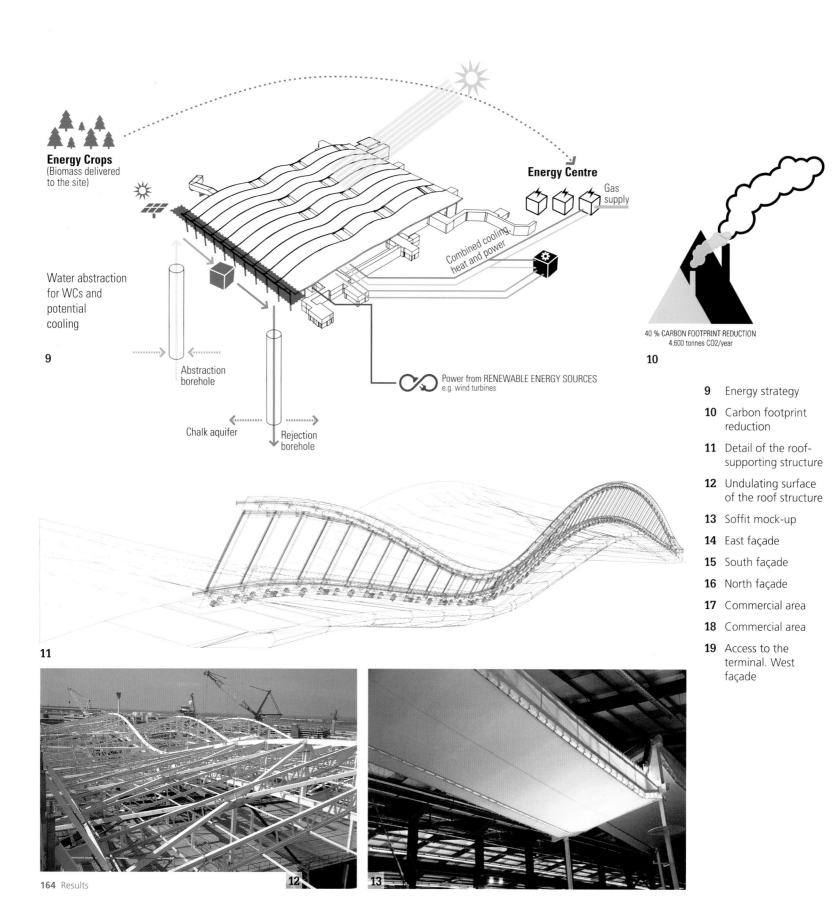

Energy Crops
(Biomass delivered to the site)

Energy Centre

Gas supply

Combined cooling, heat and power

Water abstraction for WCs and potential cooling

9

Abstraction borehole

Chalk aquifer

Rejection borehole

Power from RENEWABLE ENERGY SOURCES
e.g. wind turbines

40 % CARBON FOOTPRINT REDUCTION
4.600 tonnes CO2/year

10

9 Energy strategy

10 Carbon footprint reduction

11 Detail of the roof-supporting structure

12 Undulating surface of the roof structure

13 Soffit mock-up

14 East façade

15 South façade

16 North façade

17 Commercial area

18 Commercial area

19 Access to the terminal. West façade

11

12

13

14 15 16 17 18 19

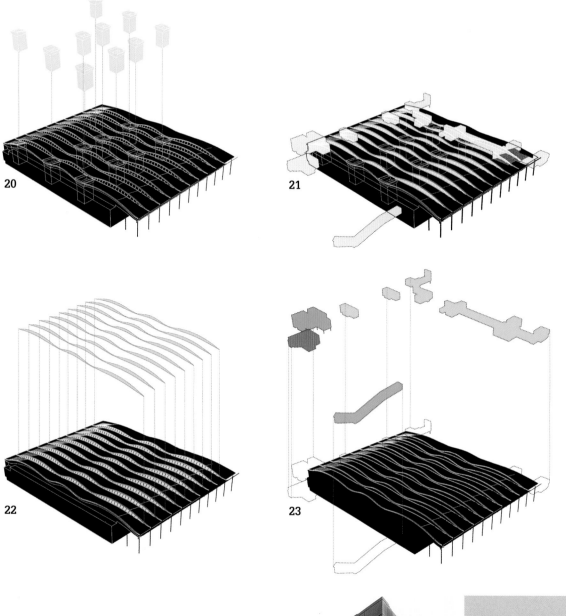

20 Service cores

21 Gates

22 Skylights

23 Gates by typology

24 FLANs on the east and south façades

25 Flexibility diagram

26 Departures routeing by passenger type

27 Arrivals routeing by passenger type

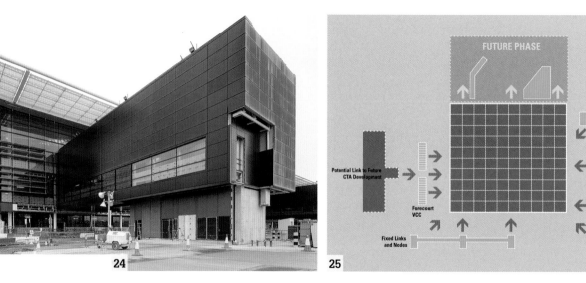

DEPARTURES /// ROUTES

———— DEPARTING PASSENGERS
———— SUPERCLASS PASSENGERS

ARRIVALS /// ROUTES

———— INTERNATIONAL PASSENGERS
———— DOMESTIC PASSENGERS
———— INTER-TERMINAL PASSENGERS
———— CTA PASSENGERS

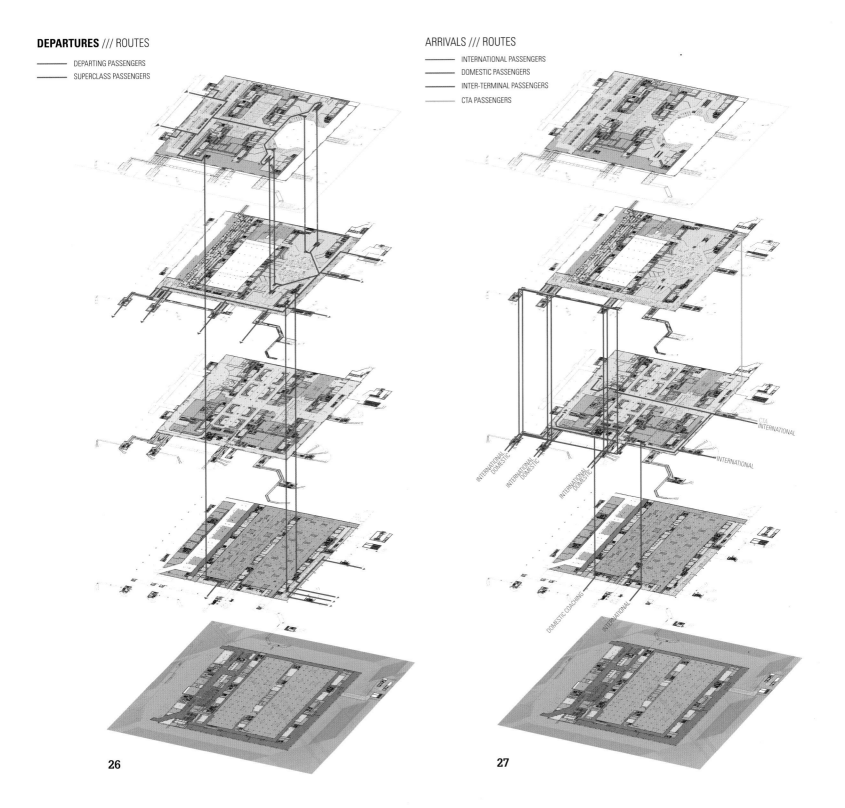

26

27

ZARAGOZA AIRPORT TERMINAL

1 Basement floorplan
2 Mezzanine floorplan
3 Ground floor plan
4 Roof plan
5 View from the entrance
6–9 Short sections
10–11 Long sections
12 Airside elevation
13 Landside elevation

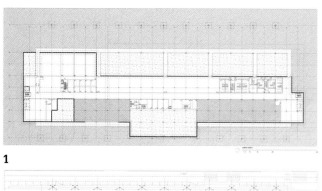

1

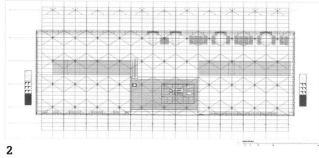

2

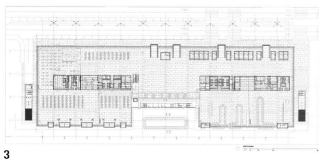

3

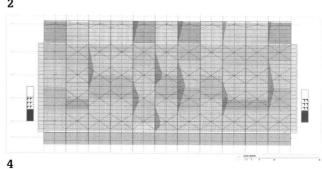

4

5

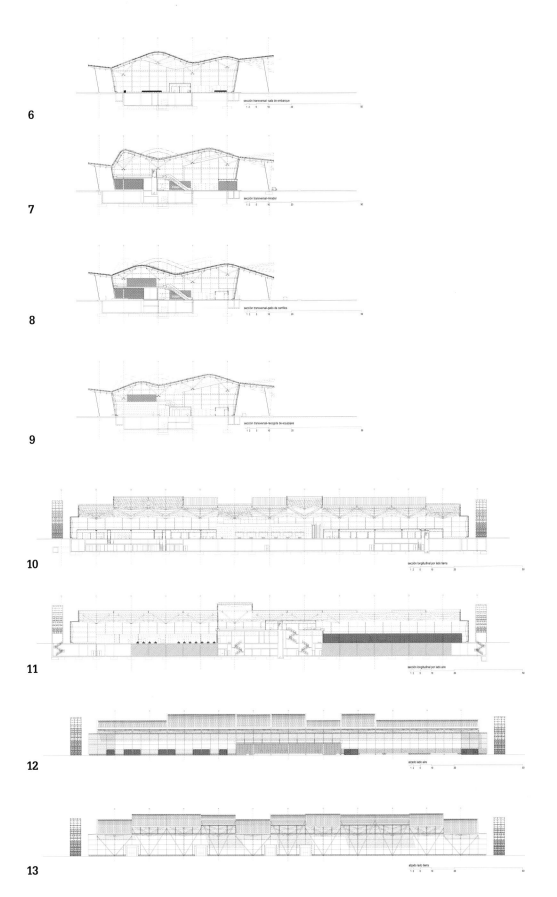

6

7

8

9

10

11

12

13

Place	Zaragoza
Date	2005–2008
Client	Spanish Airports and Air Navigation Authority (AENA)
Architects	Luis Vidal + Architects
Area	22,000sqm
Stage	Completed
Awards	First prize in international public open competition. Building finalist for the Mies van der Rohe 2009 International Prize. AENOR Energy Efficiency Certificate, 2012

Zaragoza is a city of 700,000 inhabitants, capital of the Aragon region of Spain, halfway between Madrid and Barcelona.

The purpose of the project was to develop a modern and competitive infrastructure to boost Zaragoza and to serve as a gateway during the 2008 International Expo held in Zaragoza. LVA sought not only to accommodate the international traffic generated during the Expo, but also to open up the city to European visitors, helping it to become a new tourist destination.

The terminal building responds to a simple geometry based on 11 staggered modules, which results in a wavy shape that reinforces the building's character through the roof and turns it into an icon. The design emphasizes its functionality and responds to three basic principles: flexibility (modular structure allowing a multi-stage growth), clarity (the spatial configuration follows the visitor's journey through the building) and maximization of sunlight (including roof lights in areas where passengers spend most time). The most representative and iconic element of the structure is the roof; its wavy surface reminds us of the main theme of the 2008 Expo: water and sustainable development.

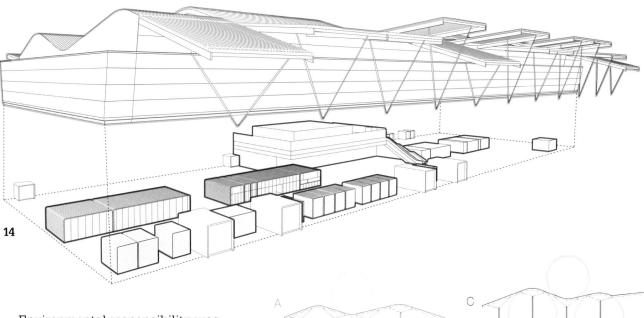

14

Environmental responsibility was a priority in the design; a simple geometry allows not only for an optimal layout but also extensive use of natural light, contributing to energy saving. A rectangular layout facilitates passenger flow and reduces waiting and circulation time, furthermore enhanced by dynamic check-in and boarding procedures. The terminal's operational areas are located on the main floor, including check-in, departures and arrivals. Offices, multi-purpose areas and a panoramic deck are located on the first floor. Outside, the landscape design seeks to preserve existing green areas through a pine reforestation plan.

15

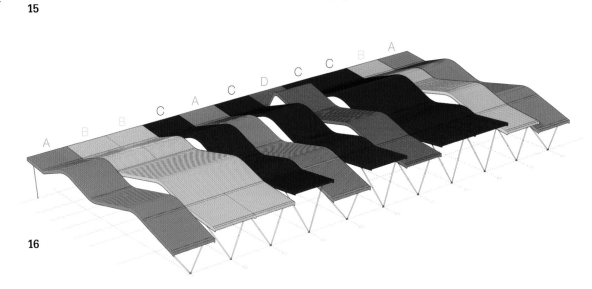

16

OFFICE COMPLEXES CAMPUS PALMAS ALTAS
FOR ABENGOA (WITH RSHP)

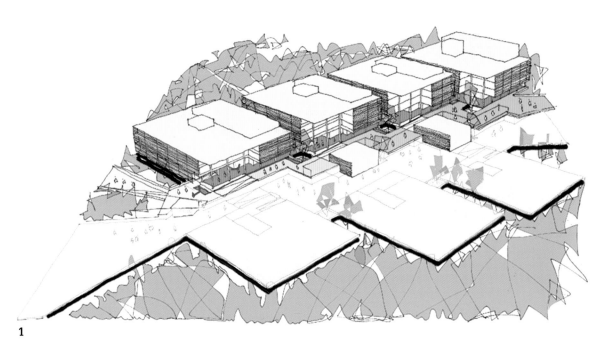

1 Higher platform
and the buildings
it serves

2 Entrance to the
campus

3 External spaces and
communal services

4 Diagrams used
during the
competition
phase to show
permeability
towards the
rivers, pedestrian
access and basic
orientation

5 View from one
of the entrance
porches

6 Interstitial spaces
between buildings

1

CAMPUS
PALMAS
ALTAS

2

Place	Seville
Date	2005–2009
Client	Abengoa
Architects	Luis Vidal + Architects / Rogers Stirk Harbour + Partners
Area	50,000sqm office space, 10,500sqm landscaped areas and courtyards and 1,300 parking spaces
Stage	Completed
Awards	First prize in a private international invitation-only competition. First building in Europe to receive LEED Platinum pre-certificate. RIBA European Award winner, 2010. Prime Property Award for sustainable development by Unino Investment Group, 2010. Design Award, Commercial Category by the American Institute of Architects, 2010

3

5

6

4

The Campus Palmas Altas, new headquarters for the Sevillan technology company Abengoa, sets new standards in sustainable architecture. Its aim is to become a real community, compact and grouped around a public space. The design therefore uses space to increase interaction between employees.

The site has a 50,000sqm buildable area, consisting of seven buildings around a main central square, designed to maximize a self-shading effect and temperature control, and 1,300 parking spaces below ground. The design team configured a system of exterior spaces, gardens and leisure areas, reflecting the vernacular Andalusian architecture and responding to seasonal weather changes.

The central square defines the site's entrance and reflects the collaborative spirit within Abengoa, acting as the main meeting place of the campus. Likewise, the scale of the buildings provides comfortable working conditions, offering natural light and ventilation, while slats in the façades control excessive light. The buildings are connected vertically, on the exterior, through an atrium performing the function of a central unifying square.

The project presents environmental technologies such as photovoltaic panels, a trigeneration plant, methanol fuel cells and efficient, sustainable HVAC (Heating, Ventilation and Air Conditioning) systems and lighting. The architects applied energy-saving criteria to every aspect, from the buildings' geometry, based on compact forms, the enveloping building's composition and the distribution and design of solar-control devices, to the choice of materials.

The result of this 'green' complex brief for Abengoa is an innovative design, which promotes exclusively pedestrian use. LVA hopes it provides a new concept for office complexes.

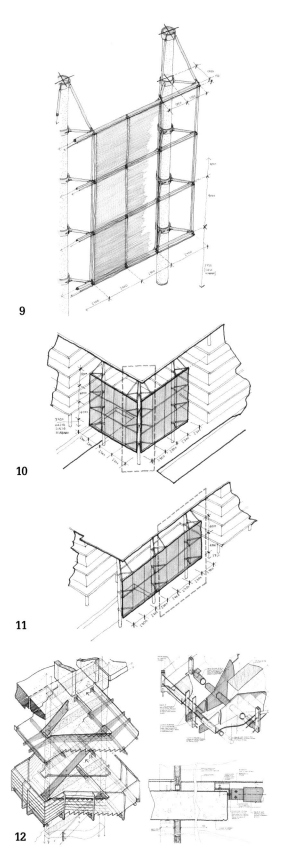

9

10

11

12

7

8

7 Trigeneration plant chimneys and entrance to the renewable energy sources exhibition

8 Courtyards bring in light to the parking area

9–11
Steel mesh marks the entrances to the buildings

12 Detailed sketches of the external fire staircases, marked out by colour

13 Night view

14 West façade and summer south sun angle

15 West façade and winter south sun angle

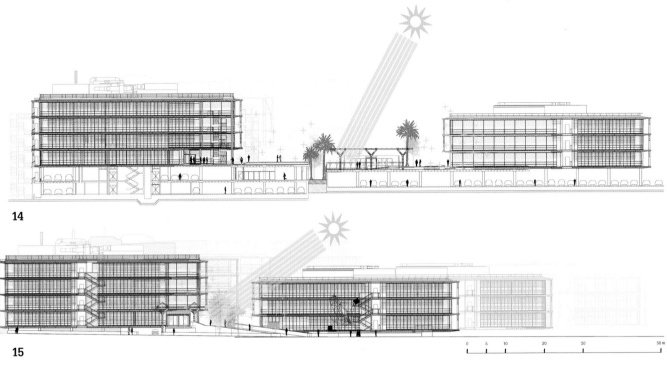

14

15

16

17

18

19

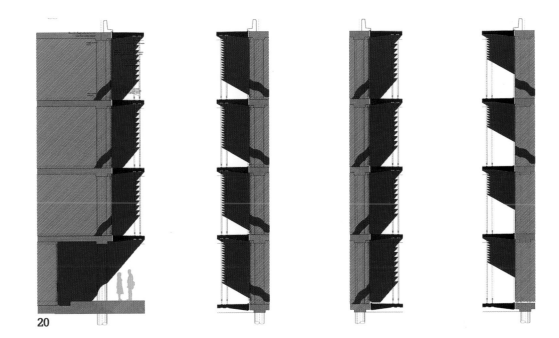

20

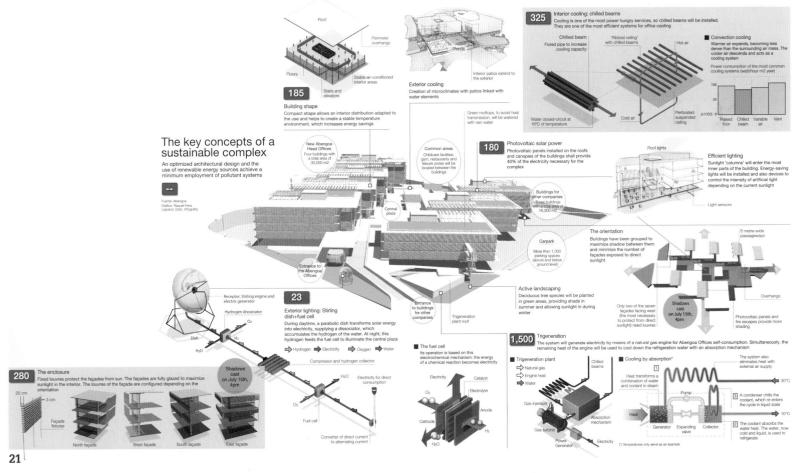

21

HOSPITALS INFANTA LEONOR HOSPITAL

1. View of satellite #2 from the car park
2. Segregation of users by floor
3. Segregation of users by floor
4. Natural light for all rooms, views out, therapeutic gardens, clear routeing and smart signage, human scale and careful use of colour
5. Colour guide
6. Six satellites around a communication spine

1

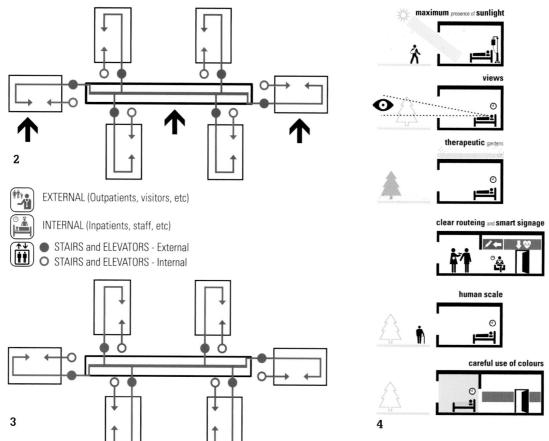

2

EXTERNAL (Outpatients, visitors, etc)

INTERNAL (Inpatients, staff, etc)

● STAIRS and ELEVATORS - External
○ STAIRS and ELEVATORS - Internal

3

4

maximum *presence of* **sunlight**

views

therapeutic *gardens*

clear routeing *and* **smart signage**

human scale

careful use of colours

Place	Vallecas (Madrid)
Date	2005–2007
Client	Madrid Regional Health Authority
Architects	Luis Vidal + Architects / Araujo + Berned
Area	130,000sqm
Facilities	204 rooms, 30 intensive care beds, 11 delivery rooms, 19 image diagnosis rooms, 141 consulting rooms, 99 emergency care beds, 13 operating theatres and 1,700 parking spaces
Stage	Completed
Awards	First prize in an open international public competition (PPP)

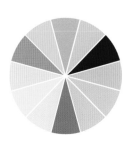

SATELLITE **#4**
I.C.U.

SATELLITE **#5**
OPERATING THEATRE

SATELLITE **#6**
EMERGENCY ROOM

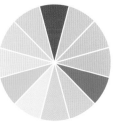

SATELLITE **#1**
OUTPATIENT CLINIC

SATELLITE **#2**
LABORATORIES

SATELLITE **#3**
X RAYS

5

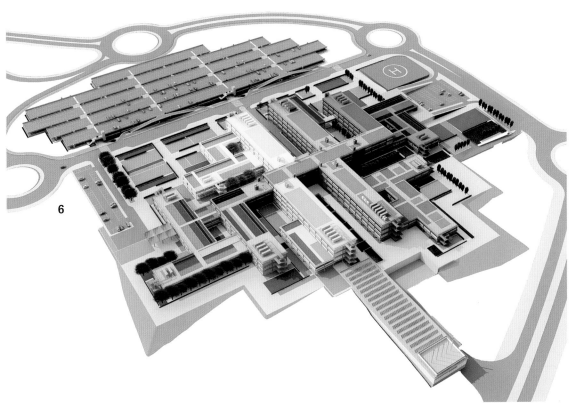

6

A new hospital typology for the twenty-first century based on two main concepts. The first is curative architecture, focused on the patient's well-being through the careful study of key aspects such as sunlight and the positive effect of therapeutic gardens (physical and visual connection). Second, the airport-hospital concept, which was developed through the experience that LVA's team gained in airport design, applying a methodology dedicated to the reduction of passenger stress and improvement of visitor experience through optimal routeing, clear pathways and direct visual connections with destinations within the building. This strategy contributes not only to the positive experience of the user but also to the optimization of the functional plan, avoiding redundant areas. It also guarantees the total segregation of flows and circulations of different groups such as staff and patients.

The building is designed to merge and fully integrate with the surroundings and has been developed using a modular scheme that allows easy extension and maximum flexibility: the building is organized along a central spine which connects six satellite buildings of different sizes and functions.

Easy orientation and legible spaces based on the circulation of hospital staff, emergency medical staff, patients and visitors are designed to avoid intersections between these groups.

Optimizing the flow of natural light into the building helps to reduce energy consumption by making use of passive heating and cooling.

This was the first hospital designed and built by LVA. This same philosophy has produced two more winning proposals so far: Can Misses (Ibiza) and Vigo (Pontevedra). Also, Infanta Leonor was one of the first examples in the world of a hospital built by PPP (public-private partnership).

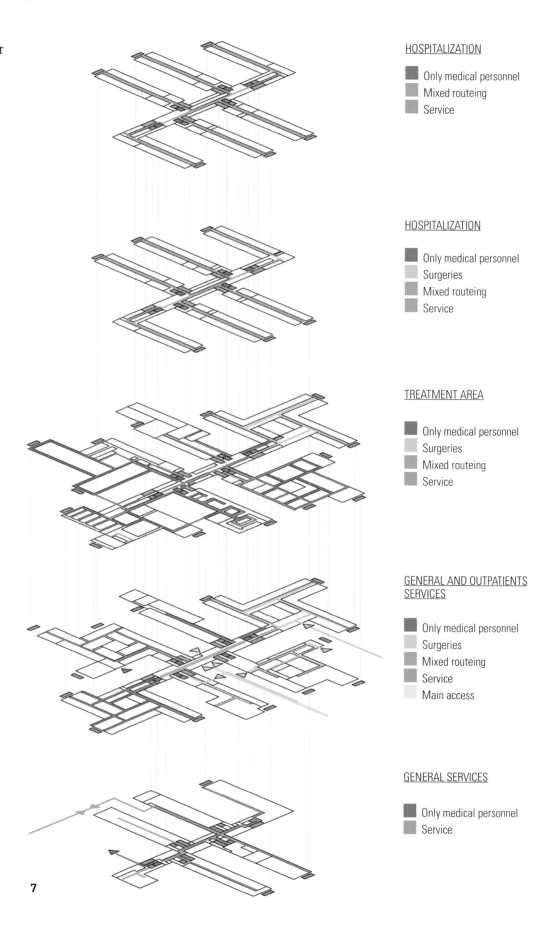

HOSPITALIZATION

- Only medical personnel
- Mixed routeing
- Service

HOSPITALIZATION

- Only medical personnel
- Surgeries
- Mixed routeing
- Service

TREATMENT AREA

- Only medical personnel
- Surgeries
- Mixed routeing
- Service

GENERAL AND OUTPATIENTS SERVICES

- Only medical personnel
- Surgeries
- Mixed routeing
- Service
- Main access

GENERAL SERVICES

- Only medical personnel
- Service

7

7 Routes inside the hospital

8 Ground floor plan

9 Green roofs

10 Courtyard

11 Space between two satellites

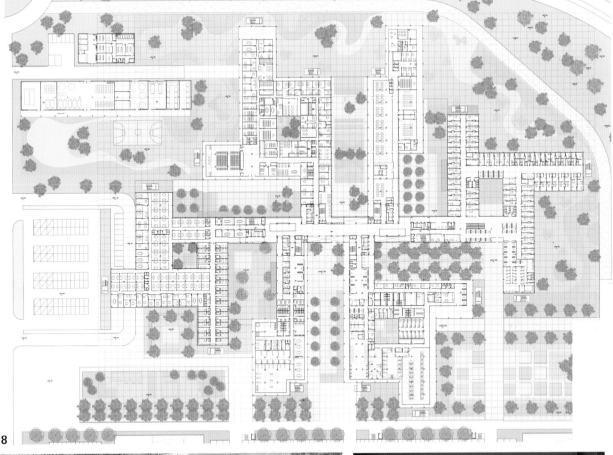

8

9

10

11

CAN MISSES HOSPITAL

1 Ward block
2 Site plan
3 Structure cantilevers in ward blocks
4 3D visualization
5 Horizontal and vertical primary communication
6 Satellites

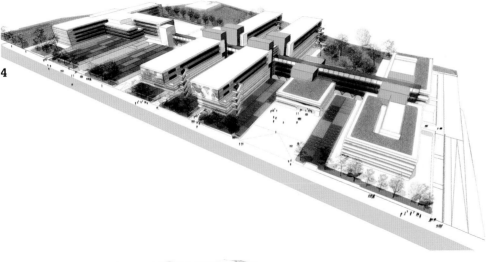

4

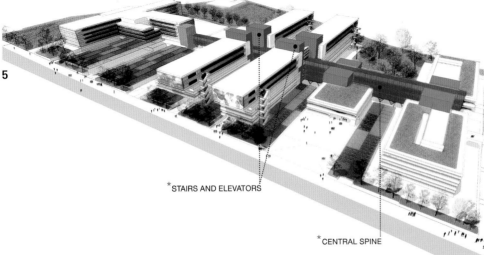

5

*STAIRS AND ELEVATORS

*CENTRAL SPINE

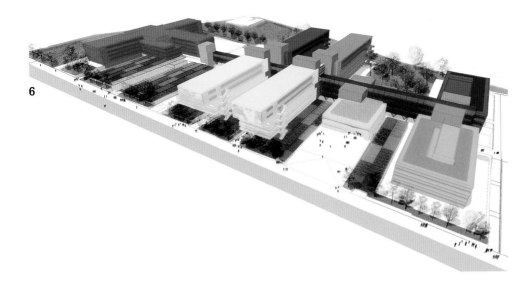

6

Place	Ibiza
Date	2008–2014
Client	Balearic Islands Regional Health Authority
Architects	Luis Vidal + Architects
Collaborations	Joint venture with Arup, D-fine and CSP
Area	50,000sqm new buildings, 25,000sqm refurbishment and 20,000sqm external spaces
Facilities	198 rooms, 23 intensive care beds, 6 delivery rooms, 19 image diagnosis rooms, 106 consulting rooms, 39 emergency care beds, 8 operating theatres and 930 parking spaces
Stage	On site
Awards	First prize in public international open competition

The island of Ibiza has a rapidly growing population of around 100,000 people, and the existing Can Misses Hospital (the only public hospital on the island) needed upgrading, expanding and modernizing.

Designed by LVA, Can Misses Hospital includes the extension for the existing building and also its internal rearrangement.

As usual in this kind of public building, the existing premises had to remain fully operational during the extension works, which required careful planning. There was also an archeological site on the land, which has been preserved and incorporated into the design.

The same design philosophy that underpinned the Infanta Leonor Hospital is behind this proposal: a new hospital conceived for twenty-first-century healthcare. In this particular case, the building was conceived to mimic Ibiza's local architecture, using a modular construction. Thus, white is the predominant colour, while thick walls and façades have well-composed openings.

Planned with sustainable-energy criteria in mind, vegetation was introduced into the hospital to provide shade and reduce the need for air-conditioning, and natural light and ventilation have been exploited where possible.

This project has been one of the first public-private partnership (PPP) schemes in the world at a working hospital. By holding face-to-face meetings with the hospital management and staff, LVA has been able to improve the circulation patterns of the existing hospital, the privacy of inpatients and the proximity of medical units, casualty department and intensive care unit, extending the philosophy from the new building to the existing one.

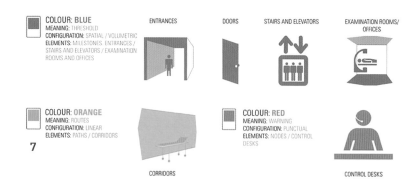

COLOUR: BLUE
MEANING: THRESHOLD
CONFIGURATION: SPATIAL / VOLUMETRIC
ELEMENTS: MILESTONES. ENTRANCES / STAIRS AND ELEVATORS / EXAMINATION ROOMS AND OFFICES

ENTRANCES · DOORS · STAIRS AND ELEVATORS · EXAMINATION ROOMS/OFFICES

COLOUR: ORANGE
MEANING: ROUTES
CONFIGURATION: LINEAR
ELEMENTS: PATHS / CORRIDORS

7

CORRIDORS

COLOUR: RED
MEANING: WARNING
CONFIGURATION: PUNCTUAL
ELEMENTS: NODES / CONTROL DESKS

CONTROL DESKS

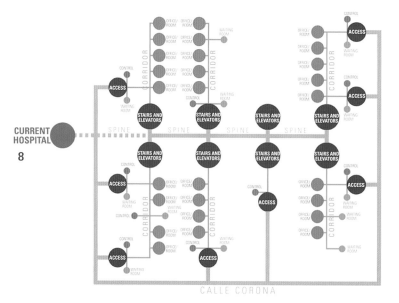

CURRENT HOSPITAL

8

CALLE CORONA

9

10

control desk and surgeries corridor

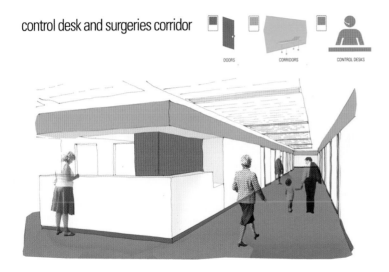

DOORS   CORRIDORS   CONTROL DESKS

surgery

EXAMINATION ROOMS/
OFFICES

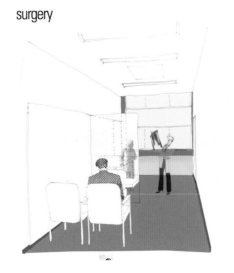

waiting room

CORRIDORS

stairs and elevators

STAIRS AND ELEVATORS

room

EXAMINATION ROOMS/
OFFICES

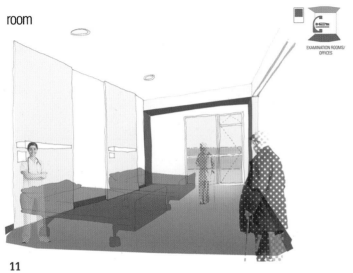

inpatients corridor

CORRIDORS   CONTROL DESKS

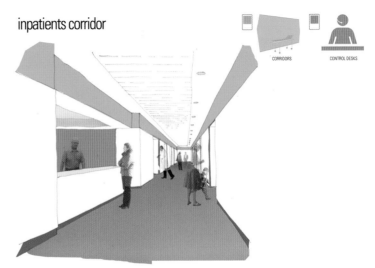

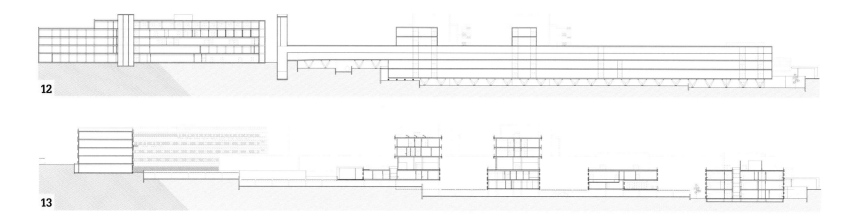

12

13

14

12 Long section
through the
communication
spine

13 Long section
through satellites

14 Spine and seven
new satellites. The
existing hospital, on
the right, became
the eighth satellite
when connected

15 Floor above main
entrance

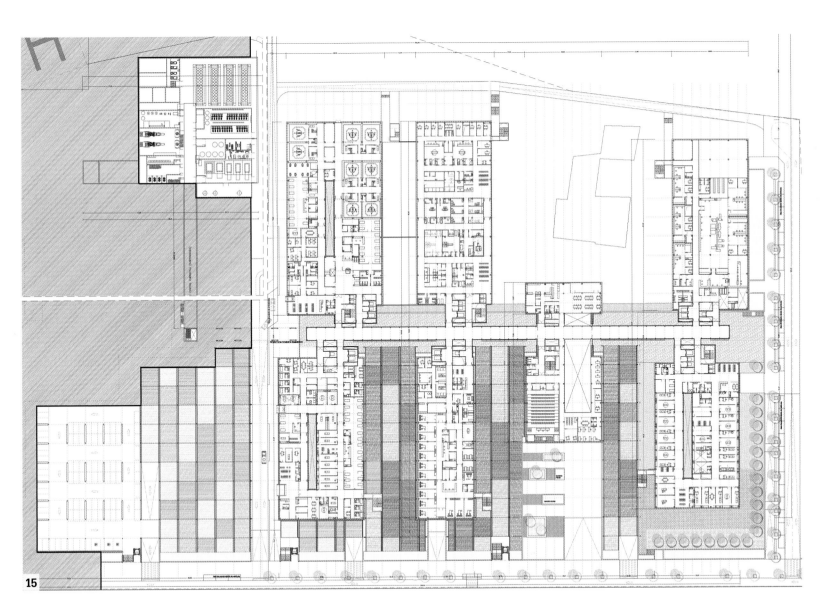

15

VIGO HOSPITAL

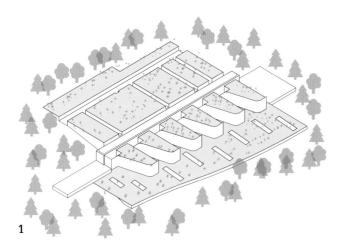

1

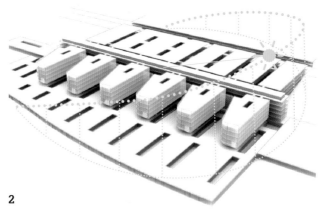

2

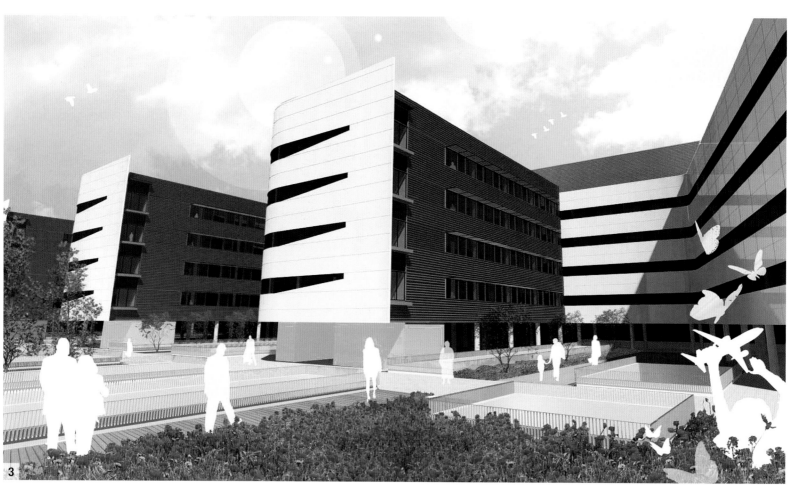

3

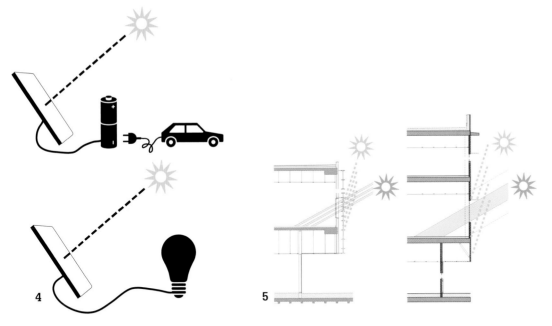

4

5

6

Place	Vigo
Date	2010–2014
Client	Galician Health Authority (SERGAS)
Architects	Luis Vidal + Architects
Collaborating architects	V. F. Couto / J. R. Losada
Contractors	Joint venture with Acciona, Puentes, Altair, Concessia and Obras y Caminos y Asfaltos
Area	170,000sqm building and 100,000sqm parking
Facilities	574 rooms, 89 intensive care beds, 12 delivery rooms, 32 image diagnosis rooms, 150 consulting rooms, 124 emergency care beds, 24 operating theatres and 4,300 parking spaces
Stage	On site
Awards	First prize in open public competition (PPP). Named Hospital of the Future 2012 at the 8th Design & Health Academy Awards, Malaysia

Vigo is a city of 300,000 inhabitants in the north-west of Spain, next to the Atlantic Ocean. With two medium-sized hospitals in the city, Vigo was in need of a bigger, newer health facility and so the health authority for the Galician region (SERGAS) launched a PPP competition. The joint venture of five construction companies commissioned LVA to design the best possible hospital on a sloped site on the outskirts of the city, within the shape and volume already determined.

As part of the brief, Vigo Hospital has to meet the requirements of twenty-first-century healthcare. LVA think this represents a step on from the conception of hospitals in the twentieth century, which was mainly based on treating inpatients. The modern hospital

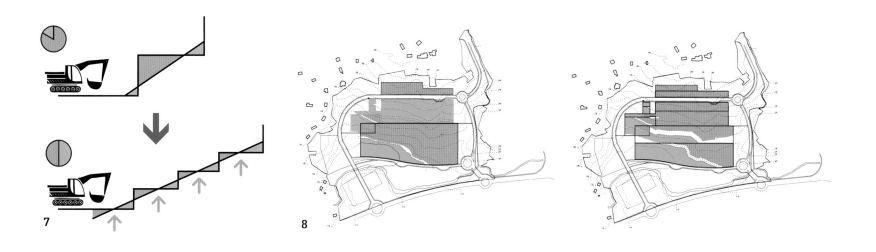

7

8

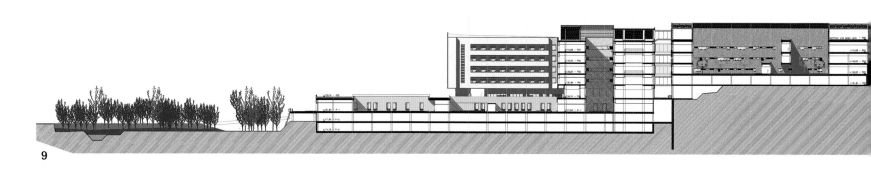

9

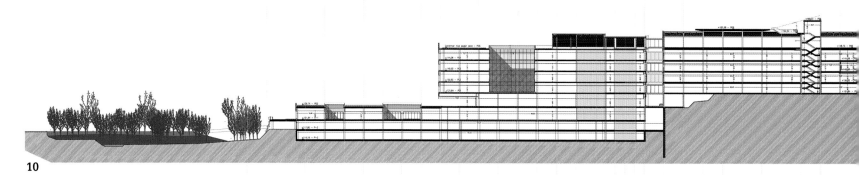

10

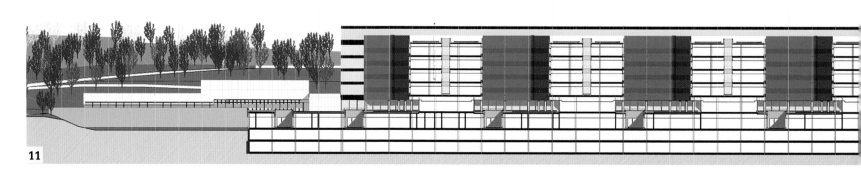

11

7 Dig-and-fill strategy

8 Dig-and-fill groundworks

9–10
Short sections

11 Long section through hospitalization blocks

12–18
The evolution of the construction works

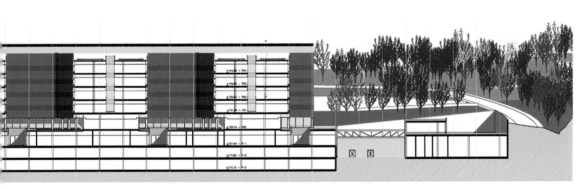

must cater for a mix of inpatients and outpatients.

Once again, the segregation of different types of user and the airport-hospital concept were the principles behind LVA's winning proposal. This time the particular constraints of the site resulted in a slightly different design. While in Infanta Leonor Hospital the spine contains working areas, and in Can Misses it is just a corridor on two levels (perhaps the most pure application of the model), in Vigo the spine is surrounded by inpatient facilities on the mountain side and outpatient care on the valley side.

The proposal is conceived with the patient's well-being in mind, and so it includes curative architecture based on sunlit spaces and a therapeutic garden designed to diminish stress.

The building fully exploits the existing slope and is terraced in the terrain, therefore creating a natural and clear division of the hospital's work. In the lower part, closest to the Barxa River, there is a stone base hosting the outpatient surgeries, above which is a large garden and public space with all principal accesses to the hospital. The six ward blocks seem to be flying over this base, allowing great views to both the valley and the garden for the inpatients. In the highest part is the technical block with specialized and emergency access.

Laminated glass brings all the elements together, cladding all vertical and horizontal communication routes, not only for the sanitary staff, patients and visitors, but also for all the building's systems.

At the time of writing, the building is under construction, and LVA is carrying out the site supervision of the architectural and civil works.

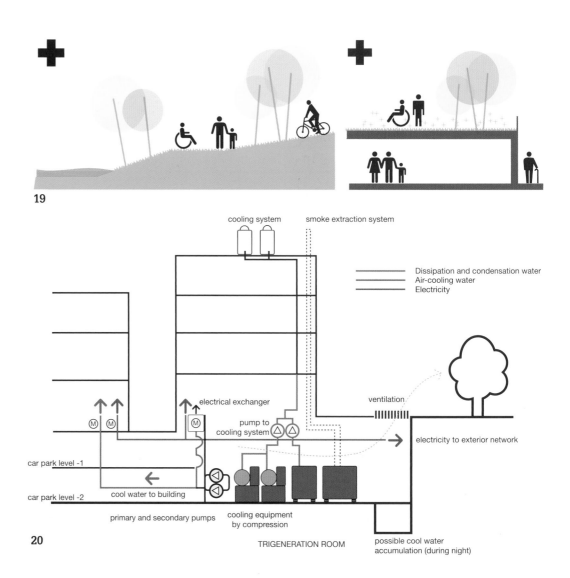

19

20

Dissipation and condensation water
Air-cooling water
Electricity

cooling system

smoke extraction system

electrical exchanger

ventilation

pump to cooling system

electricity to exterior network

car park level -1

cool water to building

car park level -2

primary and secondary pumps

cooling equipment by compression

TRIGENERATION ROOM

possible cool water accumulation (during night)

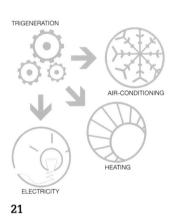

21

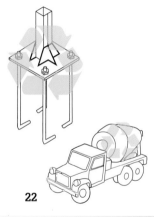

22

23

24

25

PUBLIC BUILDINGS BOTÍN CENTRE
(WITH RPBW)

Place	Santander
Date	2010–in progress
Client	Fundación Marcelino Botín
Architects	Renzo Piano Building Workshop / Luis Vidal + Architects
Area	6,000sqm
Stage	On site

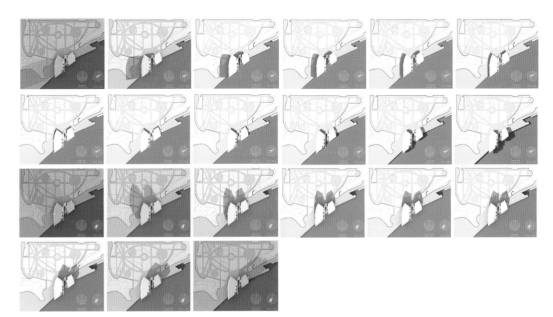

4

The Botín Centre is conceived as a new space for art and culture, an open and inclusive venue that will enrich, socially and culturally, the public life of Santander – a space destined for art, music, literature and cultural exchange.

Located in the city centre, the project, a direct commission by the client, is based on three main movements.

The first is to clear the area destined for a car park and to build a tunnel to eliminate road traffic, which isolates the plot.

The second is the enlargement of the 100-year-old Pereda Garden, doubling its area and extending it up to the shore of the bay. This will increase visual continuity between the city centre and the port.

5

6

Finally, the third movement is to 'land' this arts centre on the dock, projecting above the water, like a boat. Like a jewel floating on the seashore, it will house exhibition spaces, an auditorium and multi-purpose rooms.

Under the greyish skies of Santander, the building and its pale ceramic tiling skin, the reflected light and the lightness of the projecting volumes, bring vitality to the landscape, creating a new scenery around the bay of Santander.

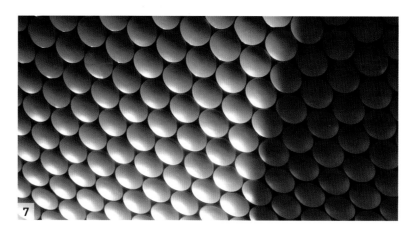

7 Ceramic buttons form the skin of the building
8 Detailed cross-section
9 Level +1
10 Level +2

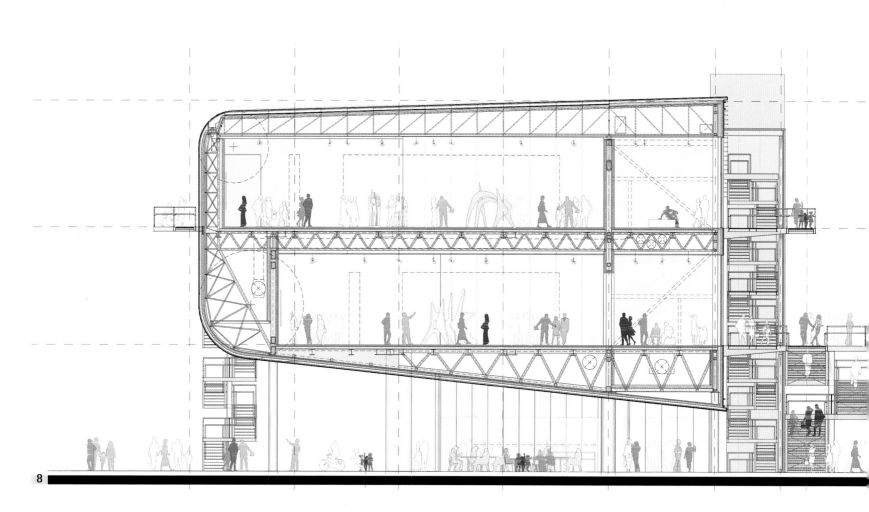

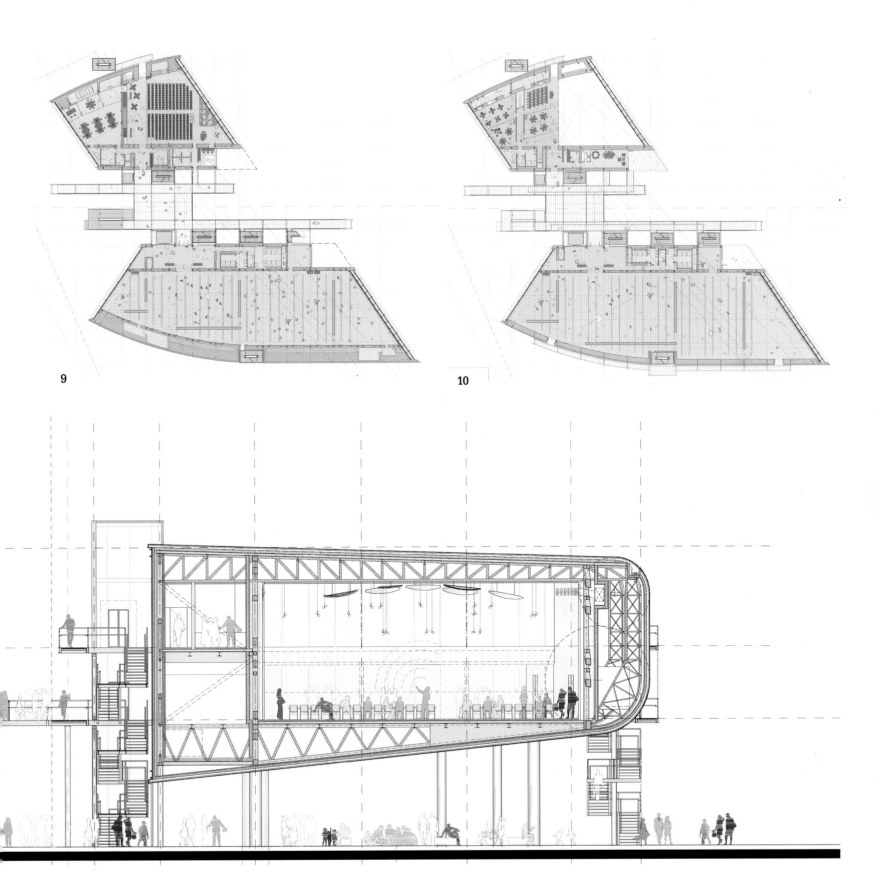

9

10

INTERIORS MNCARS RESTAURANT

1 Bar-table-bench detailed design
2 Daytime view
3 View at night
4 Central area
5 Elevation
6 Plan of the restaurant

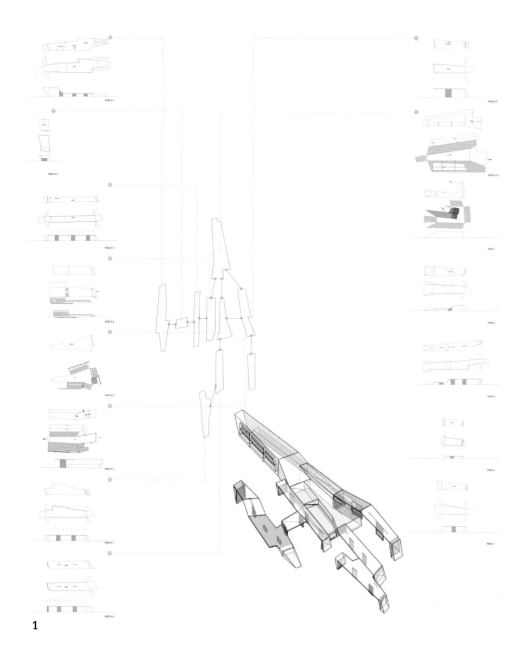

1

2

3

4

Place	Madrid
Date	2004–2005
Client	Occidental Hotels
Architects	Luis Vidal + Architects
Area	800sqm
Stage	Completed
Awards	First prize in public open international competition. Awarded best commercial establishment by Madrid City Council's 20th Architecture and Urban Planning Awards, 2005

5

6

LVA tackled the interior design of the MNCARS Restaurant in Madrid in a space conceived by architects Jean Nouvel, B-720 and Alberto Medem.

LVA's proposal was inspired by the space's own diversity, the strong presence of the iconic auditorium soffit and the need to 'colonize' the space. The design is based on the creation of an artificial topography in white 'table-bands', which contributes to the strong character of the space without competing with the distinctive building. This topography acts as a sort of carpet that folds and spreads over the space, marking the uses of various areas without hampering a view of the whole restaurant, encompassing also furniture, lighting support, tables and reading areas along its crooked length.

The table-bands, continuous and luminous, act as elements of distribution from a central strip that divides the space into a bar area and a dining area. They create micro-landscapes that allow visitors spontaneous and flexible use of the element, and hence of the space. They create an organic, changeable and versatile continuity between the furniture and the unoccupied areas of the restaurant.

ABENGOA FIT-OUT (WITH RSHP)

1

2

3

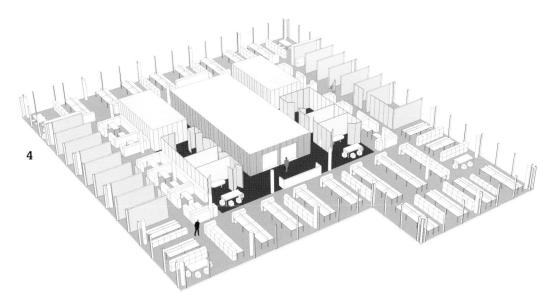

4

Place	Seville
Date	2008–2012
Client	Abengoa
Architects	Luis Vidal + Architects / Rogers Stirk Harbour + Partners
Area	36,000sqm
Stage	Completed

After the completion of the Campus Palmas Altas office in Seville (see pages 172–177), Abengoa, the owner and developer, commissioned Luis Vidal + Architects and Rogers Stirk Harbour + Partners to design the fit-out of the interiors of the four buildings (out of seven) they were to inhabit as their headquarters. This move ensured that the philosophy behind the architecture ran seamlessly into the finished product.

The interior spaces ranged from classrooms and labs to open-plan offices, semi-enclosed working cubicles, offices, informal and formal meeting spaces and coffee corners to the CEO's and Board's floors, at the top of the highest building. LVA gathered information from the different Abengoa divisions and departments.

The head office is defined by its transparent façade and open-plan interior, therefore the fit-out project sought to highlight these qualities and the building's genuine spaciousness. Besides creating a good working space, it promotes interaction between employees in the communal areas, which was one of the client's objectives.

Such criteria led the architects to design an office landscape filled with sunlight through the openings in the façade. Its luminous spaces are quiet and peaceful, creating a good atmosphere in which to work. The interiors are divided according to the

5

7

8

6

9

inherent qualities of each space, with naturally darker areas becoming private offices and lighter spaces left open-plan. This results in a flexible system that works for everyone.

One of this project's greatest achievements is that the primary architectural intentions were fulfilled by the material selection for interior finishes, furniture and signage, as well as the co-ordination and adaptation of all facilities.

CIRCULACION
CERRADOS
CELULARES (CER
ABIERTOS

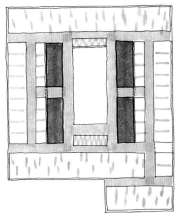

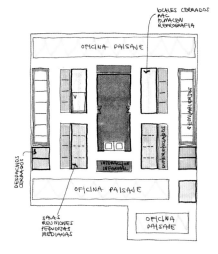

10

2

3

4

otras opciones estudiadas

11

12

13

14

15

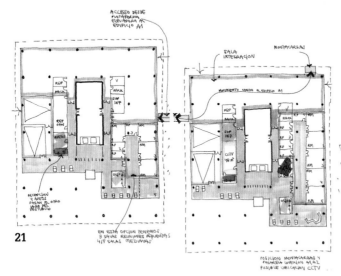

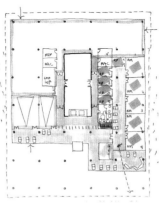

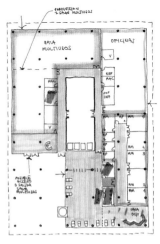

SMALLER-SCALE AND INDUSTRIAL DESIGN ABENGOA BRIDGE (WITH RSHP)

1 Site plan

2 Concept sketch

3 Elevation

4–5
Inspirational preliminary model

6 View from the access ramp

7 Detailed cross-section

8 Night view looking towards Campus Palmas Altas

9 Detail of the handrail

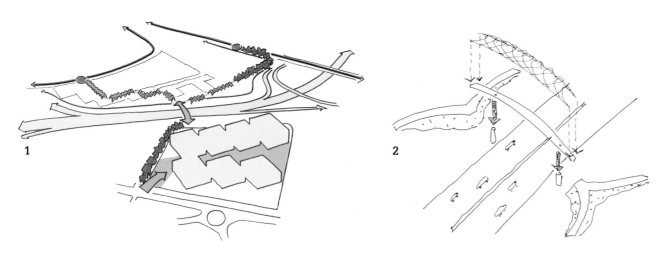

1

2

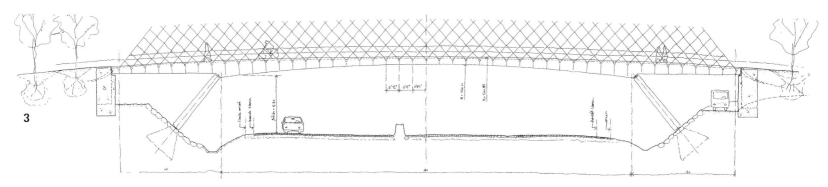

3

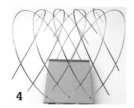

4

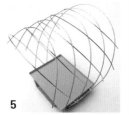

5

6

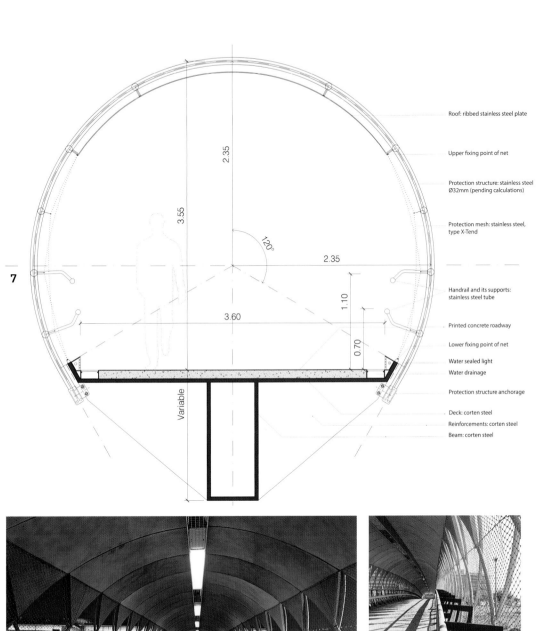

Place	Seville
Date	2009
Client	Abengoa
Architects	Luis Vidal + Architects / Rogers Stirk Harbour + Partners
Span	60m
Stage	Completed

Roof: ribbed stainless steel plate

Upper fixing point of net

Protection structure: stainless steel Ø32mm (pending calculations)

Protection mesh: stainless steel, type X-Tend

Handrail and its supports: stainless steel tube

Printed concrete roadway

Lower fixing point of net

Water sealed light

Water drainage

Protection structure anchorage

Deck: corten steel
Reinforcements: corten steel
Beam: corten steel

2.35

3.55

120°

2.35

3.60

1.10

0.70

Variable

7

8

9

Due to the economic downturn, Seville City Council delayed a subway development with a planned stop directly outside Abengoa's campus. Therefore, a safe pedestrian route from the nearest stop was needed to encourage workers to use public transport, and if it was also accessible by bicycle it could help extend the highly successful municipal bike-rental scheme, Sevici, to that part of the city.

The 60m-long bridge is perceived from inside and outside as a hollow tube, a metallic blown-up grid or net.

The detailing is fine and therefore the use of simple materials – tubes and plates – delivers an intricate play of solid and void, of light and shadow, that is elegant and subtle. As well as being aesthetically pleasing, the design offers the practical benefit of providing shelter from the sun.

Elements characteristic of engineering projects such as ramps, pillars and panels enrich the surroundings and the whole landscape. The distinctive bridge helps road users on the motorway below to recognize the campus, which therefore enhances the image of the Abengoa group.

ELECTRICITY PYLON

DESIGN **EFFICIENCY,** **MINIMIZING** THE USE OF **MATERIAL**

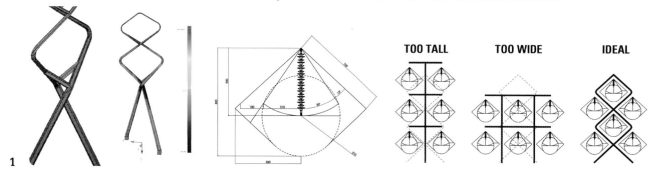

TOO TALL   TOO WIDE   IDEAL

Place	United Kingdom
Date	2011
Client	Competition run under the guidance of the Royal Institute of British Architects / National Grid (UK)
Architects	Luis Vidal + Architects
Stage	Competition

IT BLENDS INTO THE SURROUNDINGS OR STANDS AS AN ICON

FOSTERING AND IMPROVING THE LOCAL ECOSYSTEM

Designing an electricity pylon involves addressing a number of factors, including: the changing landscape it sits in; the varying colours of the different seasons; the notion of repetition of a family of elements; and the idea of communicating information and energy flow.

The design of a pylon also means taking into account the perspective of the viewer. Therefore, LVA proposed a structure that changes depending on your point of view: whether you are close or far away, whether you are moving or standing still.

The design was based on six core design principles:

- Visibility
- Flexibility
- Design efficiency
- Structural efficiency
- Ease of maintenance and durability
- Nature-friendliness

4

5

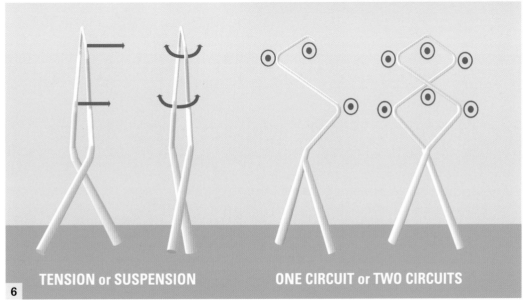

TENSION or SUSPENSION   **ONE CIRCUIT or TWO CIRCUITS**

6

MOOD SANITARYWARE FOR PORCELANOSA (WITH RSHP)

1

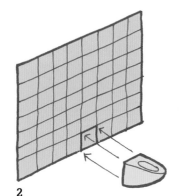 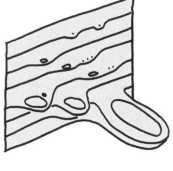 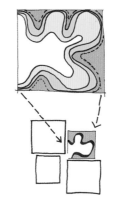 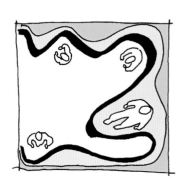

2

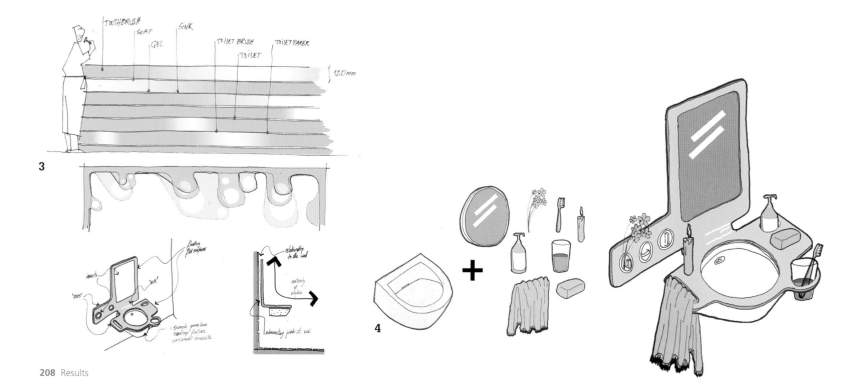

3

4

1 Types of bathroom fixture and different perceptions of them; conceptual studies

2 An almost topographical approach to design

3 Conceptual study of height for different elements

4 All-in-one concept for unity of design and ease of installation

5 Shower solution

6–8
The range is available in primary colours

5

6

7

8

Place	Madrid
Date	2010–2012
Clients	Noken and Porcelanosa Group
Architects	Luis Vidal + Architects / Rogers Stirk Harbour + Partners
Stage	On sale as MOOD sanitaryware
Awards	KBBreview Award for Innovation in Bath Products, 2013

Bathrooms have changed very little since the nineteenth century. After the incorporation of the lavatory, they evolved into a space with tiled walls and floors and porcelain sanitaryware.

From this simple definition began a bathroom-design process in which architects, their clients or the building contractors chose the ceramic elements for the walls and floor and the accessories separately. Nowadays, there is a huge range of sanitary lines and accessories, generating a 'pick 'n' mix' approach, while the spatial configuration has remained constant for years.

LVA and RSHP's concept is based on the aim of integrating the wall's surface and the sanitaryware, the two essential components in the configuration of a bathroom. Their intention was to create a small, individual space for each of the sanitary elements: bathtub, sink and toilet. The porcelain components are sober and standard, while the auxiliary elements provide enormous flexibility in terms of design and optional bathroom fittings (storage, towel racks, mirrors). Developing this concept provided not only a solution, but an infinite range of combinations and possibilities.

The analysis focused on the possibility of radically changing the composition of bathrooms; whether if by merging the expertise of both Porcelanosa and Noken, the bathroom could be reinvented.

MOOD ECO-TAP FOR PORCELANOSA

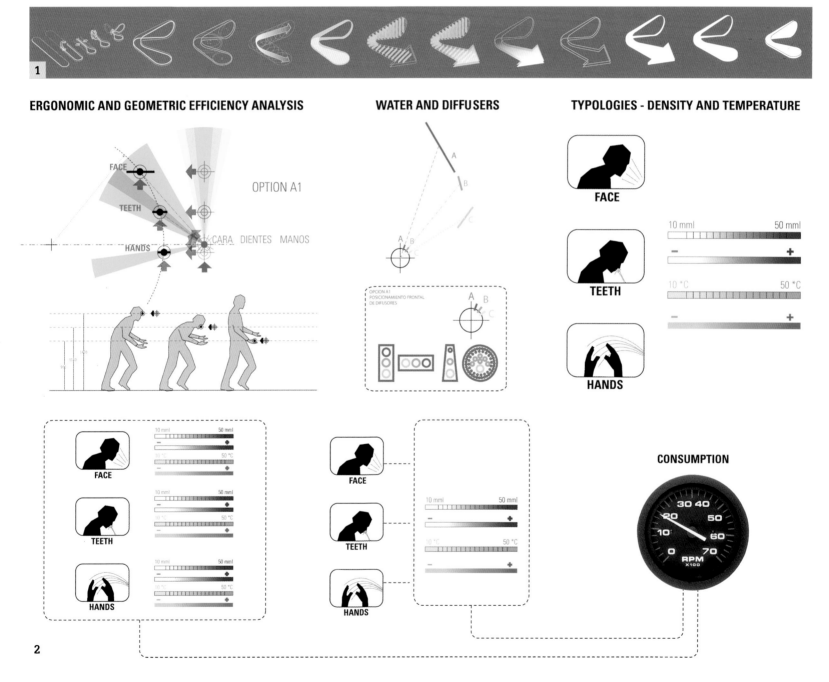

ERGONOMIC AND GEOMETRIC EFFICIENCY ANALYSIS

OPTION A1

FACE

TEETH

HANDS

CARA   DIENTES   MANOS

WATER AND DIFFUSERS

OPCION A1
POSICIONAMIENTO FRONTAL
DE DIFUSORES

TYPOLOGIES - DENSITY AND TEMPERATURE

FACE

TEETH

HANDS

10 mml   50 mml

10 °C   50 °C

FACE

TEETH

HANDS

FACE

TEETH

HANDS

CONSUMPTION

1 Geometrical
development
studies

2 Concept and
features

3 Detail of the user
interface unit

4 Mechanical version
of the tap

5 Digital version in
white

Place	Madrid
Date	2007–2012
Clients	Noken and Porcelanosa Group
Architects	Luis Vidal + Architects
Stage	On sale as MOOD brassware
Awards	KBBreview Award for Innovation in Bath Products, 2013

MOOD is a new family of brassware by LVA, including shower, bath and basin taps. The tap was inspired by water flows in nature and aims to improve the experience of domestic water use. MOOD stands out due to its geometric originality. The tap radiates simplicity and integrity, and its straightforward lines create an immediate emotional attraction, inviting you to start interacting with it. The flat spout allows for a better water flow and hides the aerator, creating a more natural feel.

The digitally controlled tap has two modes: 'sleep' (off) and 'awake' (on). In awake mode, a series of luminous icons invite the user to navigate through different options in an intuitive way. The preset functions (programmed) allow each user to personalize the water experience according to their own needs, for example face-washing or teeth-brushing. Temperature, flow and spray can be adjusted and memorized in the device. The amount of water consumed and its cost can be seen on the screen.

The design has been developed to offer an intuitive and straightforward handling by the user, while the emotional icons humanize digital technology, ensuring a perfect water experience.

3

4

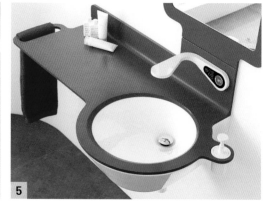

5

LVA'S KEY PEOPLE

Contributors to this book marked in **bold**

Alba del Castillo

Alfredo Biosca

Aldana Zabala

Alejandra Alonso

Alicia Castillo

Almudena Pérez

Álvaro Martínez

Álvaro Mayoral

Amparo Galván

Ana Belén Franco

Ana Claudia Mantovani

Ana Mª Prieto

Ana Marco

Ana Serrano

Andoni Arrizabalaga

Andrés Infantes

Ángela Rodríguez

Ariadna Arranz

Arturo López-Bachiller

Arturo Romero

Asier Aurrekoetxea

Bárbara Pérez

Beatriz Barco

Beatriz Llorente

Beatriz Sendín

Begoña de Andrés

Carlos Jiménez

Carlos Peña

Carmen Rivero

Carolina Hernández

Cecilia Piñeiro

Claudia García-Nieto

Claudio Balluff

Cristina Chaves

Cristina D'Cotta

Cristina Fernández

David Ávila

David Fernández Llompart

David Fernández Feito

David López

David Palomares

David Pérez

David Sobrino

Diana Martínez

Elisa Martínez

Emilio García

Enrique Pérez

Esther Crespo

Eva Clark

Eva Couto

Fernando Callejón

Florian Graumann

Francisco Rojo

Francisco Sanjuán

Gentaro Shimada

Gonzalo Fidalgo

Guillermo Martínez

Guillermo Mascort

Héctor Orden

Humberto Martínez

Icíar de Basterrechea

Ignacio Álvarez-Monteserín

Ignacio Mery

Irene Capote

Irene Méndez

Irene Rojo

Isabel Gil

Itziar Lamy

Jaime Gimeno

Javier Aguirre

Javier Palacios

Javier Torrado

Javiera Riquelme

Jean Pierre Casillas

João Abreu

José Braulio Vega

José Carlos González

José Cortines

José Luis Fernández-Morais

José Luis Lleó

José Parejo

José Gad Peralta

Jugatx López

Julio Isidro Lozano

Laura Belmonte

Laura Herreros

Lola Magaz

Lourdes Moreno

Luis Colino

Luis Vidal

Luz Mejía

Magdalena García de Durango

Manuel Navarro

Manuel Sánchez de Ocaña

Manuel Villanueva

Marcin Koltunski

Marcos Velasco

María Álvarez-Santullano

María Astiaso

María López

María Navascués

María Mosquera

María Ortega

Mario Castillo

Marta Cumellas

Martina Rauhut

Miguel Ángel Mellado

Mónica Villalba

Montserrat Ruiz

Naira Pérez

Nick Axel

Nima Haghighatpour

Nuria Martínez

Óscar Ignacio Encabo

Óscar Torrejón

Pablo Vila

Paloma Martín

Patricia Allona

Patricia Lozano

Patricia Rojas

Paz Armenta

Pedro Portillo

Raquel Albarrán

Raúl Gómez

Raúl Torres

Reyes León

Roberta Sartori

Rocío Martín

Rosa Alonso

Silvia Martín

Sol Uriarte

Sonia Ferreras

Sonia Gutiérrez

Sonia Meléndez

Sonia Pérez

Susana Sastre

Susanne Forner

Teresa Serrano

Vanessa Oleart

Verónica van Kesteren

Zelia da Costa

LVA'S FRIENDS

Clients, Consultants and Friends who have contributed to this book

Anna Giró
dosAdos Landscape Architecture

Arturo Berned
Sculptor

Chris Dawson
Architect

Eladio Cuiña
President of INASUS

Steve Riojas
Senior Vice-President at HDR Architects

Ignacio Fernández
Façade consultant at ARUP

Isabel Pascual
LVA communications

Janet Kafka
International business owner
and Honorary Consul of Spain

Joaquín Ibáñez and Maví Pérez-Maffei
Clients

José Manuel Hesse
Aeronautical Engineer

Juan Antonio Cantalapiedra
Urbespacios

Juan López-Ibor
Clínica López-Ibor, CEO

Lennart Grut
Partner at Rogers Stirk Harbour + Partners

María Arboledas
NH Hoteles EMEA Projects Director

Raymond Hole
Founder of Ray Hole Architects

Richard Rogers
Chairman at Rogers Stirk Harbour + Partners

Simon Smithson
Partner at Rogers Stirk Harbour + Partners

BIBLIOGRAPHY

Augé, M., 1996, 'About non-places', in Melhuish, C., ed., *Architecture and Anthropology*, AD Profile 124. London: Academy Editions, 82–83

Binney, M., 1999, *Airport Builders*. Chichester: Academy Editions

Brain, D., and Crane, D., 1994, 'Cultural production as "society in the making": architecture as an exemplar of the social construction of cultural artefacts', in Crane, ed., *The Sociology of Culture*. Oxford: Blackwell

Brand, S., 1995, *How Buildings Learn: What Happens after they're Built*. New York: Penguin

Callon, M., 1996, 'Le travail de la conception en architecture', in *Situations: Les cahiers de la recherche architecturale* 37, 25–35

Cuadra, M., 2002, *World Airports*. Hamburg: Junius Verlag

Elsheshtawy, Y., 2010, *Dubai: Behind an Urban Spectacle*. London: Routledge

Farias, I., 2010, 'Introduction: decentring the object of urban studies', in Farias, and Bender, T., eds, *Urban Assemblages: How Actor-network Theory Changes Urban Studies*. London: Routledge

Frampton., K., 1980, *Modern Architecture: A Critical History*. London: Thames and Hudson

Hirsch, E., and O'Hanlon, M., eds, 1996, *The Anthropology of Landscape: Perspectives on Place and Space*. Oxford: Clarendon Press

Itten., J., 1974 [1920], *The Art of Colour: The Subjective Experience and Objective Rationale of Colour*. Chichester: John Wiley

James, P., and Noakes, T., 1994, *Hospital Architecture*. London: Longman

Jenkins, L., 2002, '11, Rue de conservatoire and the permeability of buildings', in *Space and Culture* 5:3, 222–236

Lonsway, B., 2009, *Making Leisure Work: Architecture and the Experience Economy*. London: Routledge

Marcus, G., and Okely, J., 2007, 'How short can fieldwork be?' in *Social anthropology / Anthropologie sociale* 15:3, 353–367

Melhuish, C., 1993, 'Colour and architecture', in *Building Design* 26.2.1993. An exhibition at the RIBA Heinz Gallery, London

Melhuish, C., 2006, *The Life and Times of the Brunswick*. London: Camden History Society

Newton, I., 2007 [1704], *Opticks: Treatise of the Reflections, Refractions, Inflections & Colours of Light*. New York: Cosimo Classics

Nippert-Eng, C., 1996, *Home and Work: Negotiating Boundaries through Everyday Life*. Chicago: Chicago University Press

OMA (Koolhaas, R., and Mau, B.), 1995, *SMLXL*. New York: Monacelli Press

Parisi, L., 2009, 'Symbiotic architecture: prehending digitality', in *Theory Culture and Society* 26:2–3, 346–374

Ren, X., 2011, *Building Globalization: Transnational Architecture Production in Urban China*. Chicago and London: University of Chicago Press

Riley, T., 2006, *On-Site: New Architecture in Spain*. New York: Museum of Modern Art (exhibition catalogue)

Sassen, S., 2012 [1994], *Cities in a World Economy*. Thousand Oaks and London: Pine Forge Press

Taut, B., 1925, 'The rebirth of colour', manifesto, in Duttman, Schmuck, Uhl, eds, 1981, *Colour in Townscape: Handbook in Six Parts for Architects, Designers and Contractors, for City-dwellers and other Observant People*. London: Architectural Press

Tilley, C., 1994, 'Space, place, landscape and perception: phenomenological perspectives', in Tilley, *A Phenomenology of Landscape*. Oxford: Berg, 7–34

Vidal, L., 2011, 'Collective responsibility in Europe'. Exhibition at European Parliament, Brussels

Wagenaar, C., ed., 2006, *The Architecture of Hospitals*. Rotterdam: NAi.

Yaneva, A., 2009, 'Reconnecting practice and meaning', in RIBA Research Symposium Changing Practices

Interviews with Luis Vidal and other members of the office conducted in Madrid in December 2011 and March 2012

Interviews with Heathrow team conducted in London in April 2012 and with Óscar Torrejón in November 2012

Interviews with Richard Rogers and Simon Smithson conducted in March 2012

INDEX

Figures in *italics* refer to picture captions

PICTURE CREDITS

Thanks to the following for the use of images in this book. All other images courtesy Luis Vidal + Architects.

Pages 2–3 © LHR Airports Limited see photolibrary.heathrow.com; page 4 right Miguel de Guzmán; page 5 left Víctor Sájara; page 5 right © LHR Airports Limited see photolibrary.heathrow.com.

Introduction
Pages 8 and 10 Video by Javier Lorenzo; pages 14–15 © LHR Airports Limited see photolibrary.heathrow.com; page 16 both Juan Roldán; page 17 above Javier Lorenzo; page 17 below Chema Conesa; page 20 © LHR Airports Limited see photolibrary.heathrow.com; page 22 top and centre Marta Cumellas; page 22 below left and right Javier Lorenzo; page 24 Víctor Sájara; page 26 left Video by Javier Lorenzo; page 26 right Stephen Barrett; page 27 left Diario de Valladolid / Diego Sinova; page 28 Gentaro Shimada; page 29 Juan Roldán; page 30 Víctor Sájara; page 35 below María Astiaso; page 37 below Library of Congress / Wilbur and/or Orville Wright.

Design as an open-ended process
Page 40 top and page 41 Juan Roldán; page 42 below Baggage Trolley designed by Fredrik Jansson from The Noun Project; page 49 above Luis Vidal; page 50 top Dinosaur designed by Kyle Sasquie Klitch from The Noun Project; page 51 above Juan Laguna; pages 52–53 Miguel de Guzmán; page 54 above left and below Diario de Valladolid / Diego Sinova; page 55 right Chema Conesa; page 55 below left Simon Smithson; page 57 above Miguel de Guzmán; page 61 both Víctor Sájara; pages 64–65 © LHR Airports Limited see photolibrary.heathrow.com; page 67 above and below right Juan Roldán; page 68 Miguel de Guzmán; page 71 left Juan Roldán; page 73 right Miguel de Guzmán; page 74 Miguel de Guzmán; page 75 Xavier Durán; pages 76–77 Juan Roldán; page 78 Miguel de Guzmán; page 84 Mark Bentley; page 85 Víctor Sájara; page 87 left Víctor Sájara; page 93 centre Juan Roldán; pages 94 and 95 Víctor Sájara;

page 96 top Mónica Villalba de Madariaga; page 96 centre left Tree designed by Valentina Piccione from The Noun Project; page 96 bottom Piggy bank designed by Brock Kenzler from the Noun Project; page 97 both Arup; pages 98 and 99 Víctor Sájara.

Design leading to results
Page 106 all Marta Cumellas; page 110 left Javier Lorenzo; page 113 above Drink designed by Alessandro Suraci from the Noun Project; page 113 below right Simon Smithson; page 115 below Diario de Valladolid / Diego Sinova; page 117 below Javier Lorenzo; page 129 © LHR Airports Limited see photolibrary.heathrow.com; page 130 top Stephen Barrett; pages 132 top, 133, 134 below, 136 both and 137 above © LHR Airports Limited see photolibrary.heathrow.com; page 138 below right Javier Lorenzo; pages 141 and 143 both © LHR Airports Limited see photolibrary.heathrow.com; page 144 Eduardo López-Jamar.

Results
Pages 160 above, 162 both, 163 above left and right, 165 top left, centre left and right, bottom left and right and 166 bottom left © LHR Airports Limited see photolibrary.heathrow.com; pages 168 bottom and 171 top right and bottom left Miguel de Guzmán; page 171 centre left and bottom right Juan Roldán; pages 172 below, 173 below left and right, 174 left and centre, 175 top and 176 above left and below left and right Víctor Sájara; page 176 above right Mark Bentley; page 177 below Diario de Sevilla; pages 178 above and 181 below left and bottom right Miguel de Guzmán; page 181 centre right Juan Roldán; pages 182 above and 186 bottom Xavier Durán; page 191 all Tafyr.es; pages 200 all, 201, 202 and 203 all photographs, 204 bottom right and 205 below left and right Víctor Sájara.

Pages 214–215 Mónica Villalba de Madariaga; page 224 Pablo Vidal Rojas.

NOTE FROM THE CREATIVE DIRECTOR

I would like to thank Luis Vidal and Óscar Torrejón for trusting me to lead this project and letting me go ahead with my crazy ideas.

I would like to thank Clare Melhuish, Philip Cooper, Clare Double and John Round for their patience with such an inexperienced editor as myself.

I would like to thank Mónica Villalba for her invaluable help in managing the image files, for drawing beautiful diagrams and for giving good advice.

I would like to thank each of the 30 contributors for their comments.

It has been fun to work with you.
When is the next one?

MARTA CUMELLAS

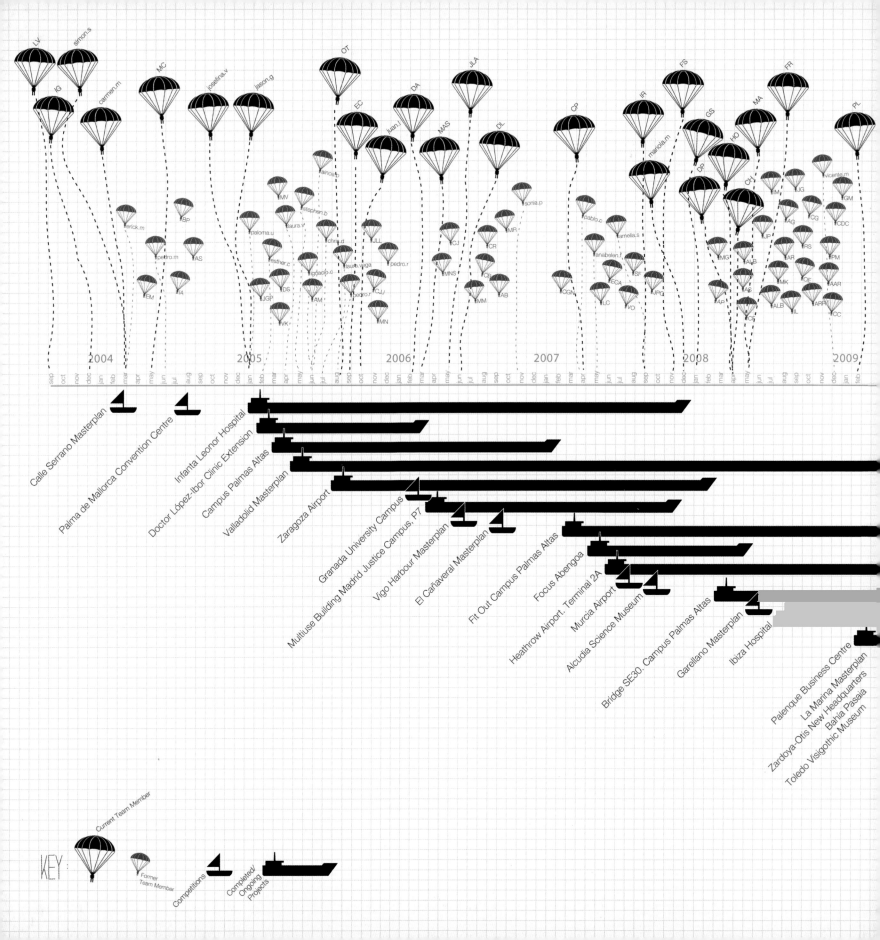

KEY:
Current Team Member
Former Team Member
Competitions
Completed/ Ongoing Projects

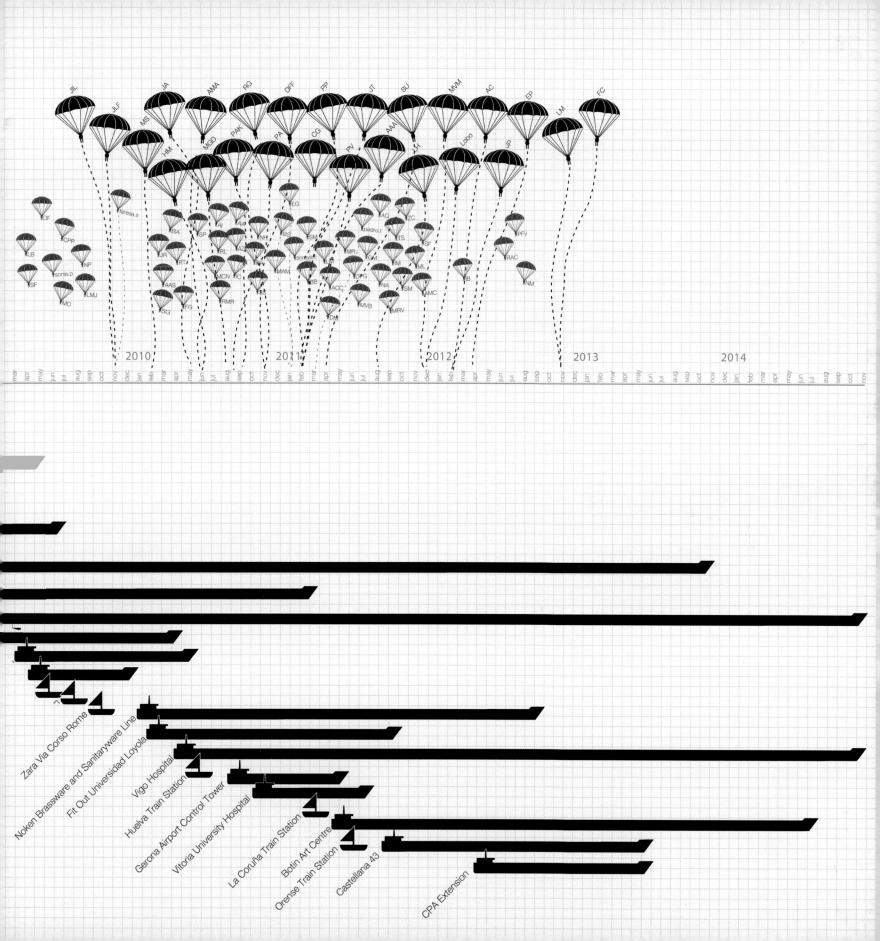

2010   2011   2012   2013   2014

Zara Via Corso Rome
Noken Brassware and Sanitaryware Line
Fit Out Universidad Loyola
Vigo Hospital
Huelva Train Station
Gerona Airport Control Tower
Vitoria University Hospital
La Coruña Train Station
Botín Art Centre
Orense Train Station
Castellana 43
CPA Extension

ACKNOWLEDGEMENTS

Nothing of what appears in this book would have happened if it were not for my Partners.

First of all, my Life Partner, Patricia, also my wife and the mother of our three sons, who has unconditionally supported me throughout all these years.

Patricia has the power to move mountains, align wishes, surpass cliffs and achieve success. She is intelligent, determined, proactive and the best possible ally any human being could dream for.

Richard Rogers and his 10 Directors, including Simon Smithson and Lennart Grut, have been without doubt my best Business Partners. They have always trusted me, listened to what I had to say and together we have accomplished many great projects which will stand for many decades.

Marta Cumellas and Óscar Torrejón, my Practice Partners, alongside Associates like Isabel Gil, Jugatx López, Francisco San Juan and Francisco Rojo, who have since day one been loyal, committed, have motivated all our team and always delivered to our clients projects that fulfil our motto: we give more for less. And a huge Thank You to all members of the teams that have worked in LVA.

Thank you to all of you, but also a big thanks to all our best clients, consultants and friends. Without all of you great buildings cannot be delivered.

LUIS VIDAL